SpringerBriefs in Computer Science

SpringerBriefs present concise summaries of cutting-edge research and practical applications across a wide spectrum of fields. Featuring compact volumes of 50 to 125 pages, the series covers a range of content from professional to academic.

Typical topics might include:

- A timely report of state-of-the art analytical techniques
- A bridge between new research results, as published in journal articles, and a contextual literature review
- A snapshot of a hot or emerging topic
- An in-depth case study or clinical example
- A presentation of core concepts that students must understand in order to make independent contributions.

Briefs allow authors to present their ideas and readers to absorb them with minimal time investment. Briefs will be published as part of Springer's eBook collection, with millions of users worldwide. In addition, Briefs will be available for individual print and electronic purchase. Briefs are characterized by fast, global electronic dissemination, standard publishing contracts, easy-to-use manuscript preparation and formatting guidelines, and expedited production schedules. We aim for publication 8–12 weeks after acceptance. Both solicited and unsolicited manuscripts are considered for publication in this series.

**Indexing: This series is indexed in Scopus, Ei-Compendex, and zbMATH **

Trish O'Connell

Trust in Agile Teams

Unlocking the Hidden Catalyst of Agile Success

Springer

Trish O'Connell
School of Science and Computing
Atlantic Technological University (ATU)
Galway, Ireland

ISSN 2191-5768 ISSN 2191-5776 (electronic)
SpringerBriefs in Computer Science
ISBN 978-3-032-21962-6 ISBN 978-3-032-21963-3 (eBook)
https://doi.org/10.1007/978-3-032-21963-3

This Springer imprint is published by the registered company Springer Nature Switzerland AG
The registered company address is: Gewerbestrasse 11, 6330 Cham, Switzerland

This book is dedicated to my husband, Dave,
and
our children, Aoife and Eoghan, with love.

Preface

Trust is frequently cited as a critical condition for effective collaboration in Agile Scrum teams. It is commonly invoked as a prerequisite for knowledge sharing, self-organisation and collective responsibility, yet it is rarely examined in any depth. While Scrum literature consistently emphasises the importance of trust, the concept itself often remains implicit i.e. assumed rather than clearly defined, theorised or operationalised within the Scrum framework.

This book responds to that gap by examining trust in Scrum as a socially constructed phenomenon that underpins autonomy, collaboration and sustained agile performance. It is based on the author's Ph.D. doctoral thesis which presented a constructivist grounded theory based on qualitative data gathered from Scrum practitioners working within major blue-chip multinational software development organisations. The analysis is informed by practitioners lived experiences of agile software development and by the author's many years of experience leading and managing teams, alongside a sustained interest in organisational dynamics and the interpersonal dynamics that enable team success. The author also holds formal certification as a Scrum Master (Certified ScrumMaster®) providing an informed grounding in Scrum principles and practices.

The book develops a multi-layered exploration of trust in agile contexts. It begins by positioning trust as foundational to Agile ways of working, tracing the shift from command-and-control models towards trust-based autonomy and self-organisation. It then examines trust through both cognitive and affective lenses, exploring how competence, reliability, emotional bonds and psychological safety interact to shape team confidence and effectiveness. Drawing on foundational trust theories originating in the twentieth century and still central to contemporary trust research, the book connects these dimensions to agile principles, team structures and everyday practices.

Subsequent chapters explore how trust is enacted and challenged within agile teams, including its role in collaboration, knowledge sharing, feedback, learning and collective accountability. Particular attention is given to the barriers that can undermine trust, viz., role ambiguity, hierarchical power residues, communication breakdowns and distributed working conditions. More importantly practices that actively help teams navigate and overcome these challenges are presented. The book also examines how trust is cultivated and sustained at scale, in distributed and remote environments, and across culturally diverse teams, highlighting the role of leadership, communication patterns, rituals and shared meaning.

Throughout, the focus remains on trust as a practical dynamic force that shapes how teams work together over time. The book argues that whilst sustainable agility depends to some extent on Agile processes and ceremonies, true agility is based on the relational foundations that enable autonomy, interdependence, alignment and learning to coexist.

This book is intended for Scrum practitioners, Scrum masters and organisations seeking to strengthen collaboration and effectiveness in agile environments. It is also relevant to researchers interested in the social, organisational and methodological dimensions of Agile and Scrum. No prior background in software development is required, however a basic knowledge of Agile and Scrum would be helpful.

To the best of the author's knowledge, existing books on Agile software development and Scrum acknowledge trust as both critical and necessary but tend to stop short of examining the construct in any depth. By focusing explicitly on trust and its enabling conditions across individual, team and organisational levels, this book aims to complement and extend current Agile literature, offering a sustained and empirically grounded contribution to understanding how agile teams build, sustain and repair trust in practice.

Galway, Ireland Trish O'Connell

Acknowledgements This book is grounded in practical experience, scholarly inquiry and reflective engagement with practice. The author is indebted to the many Scrum masters, product owners and software developers who generously gave their time to participate in interviews and share their experiences as part of this research. These practitioners, drawn from major multinational organisations including Cisco, Ericsson, IBM, Valeo Vision Systems and Avaya, offered candid insights into both the successes and challenges of working in agile environments, forming the empirical foundation of this book.

The author would like to express sincere gratitude to Dr. Owen Molloy of the University of Galway for his academic supervision, guidance and thoughtful challenge throughout the doctoral journey from which this book emerged. His perspective, insight and timely humour were invaluable in shaping both the research and the process of completing it.

Thanks are also extended to my colleagues at Atlantic Technological University for their encouragement, collegiality and ongoing support during the development of this book.

Any remaining shortcomings are, of course, the author's own.

Competing Interests The author has no competing interests to declare that are relevant to the content of this manuscript.

Contents

Chapter 1
The Role of Trust in Agile Success

Abstract Agile frameworks have redefined software development by shifting from hierarchical control to collaborative autonomy. However, this transformation is unsustainable without trust. This chapter examines trust as the foundational enabler of Agile success, arguing that it is not merely beneficial but structurally essential. Drawing on grounded theory and empirical insights, it explores how trust underpins team autonomy, knowledge sharing, distributed leadership, and the enactment of core Scrum values such as commitment and courage. Two distinct yet interdependent dimensions of trust: cognitive, based on competence and reliability, and affective, grounded in interpersonal care and shared purpose, are analysed as critical to team cohesion and adaptability. The chapter also considers how swift trust emerges in time-constrained teams, how trust supports shared decision-making and psychological safety, and how its absence leads to superficial or dysfunctional Agile practices. Ultimately, trust is presented as the unspoken architecture that sustains high-performing, self-organising teams. Without it, Agile becomes a façade, with it, teams can innovate, adapt, and collaborate with integrity and resilience.

1.1 Introduction

Agile frameworks have transformed the way software is developed, not merely by introducing new practices, but by redefining the relational dynamics at the heart of team performance. At the centre of this transformation lies trust. While traditional models emphasised control, predictability, and hierarchical decision-making, Agile shifts the emphasis to collaboration, iteration, and decentralised authority. Yet, this shift is not sustainable without trust. Trust is the unspoken architecture that supports autonomy, facilitates shared decision-making and enables continuous improvement. Trust activates key Scrum values such as focus, respect, openness, commitment and courage. Despite its centrality, trust is often assumed rather than examined, and rarely is it operationalised with the same rigour as technical processes. This chapter explores why trust is foundational to Agile success. It describes how trust underpins team autonomy, fuels knowledge sharing, supports distributed leadership, and serves

T. O'Connell, *Trust in Agile Teams*,
SpringerBriefs in Computer Science, https://doi.org/10.1007/978-3-032-21963-3_1

as a counterbalance to traditional control mechanisms. Through these lenses, the chapter reveals that trust is both a prerequisite and a product of high-functioning Agile teams.

1.2 Why Trust is Foundational in Agile

Agile's shift in software development is relational as opposed to procedural. Unlike traditional, control-oriented models reliant on hierarchical oversight, Agile depends on trust as its cornerstone. Establishing this trust is essential for team autonomy, collaboration, and the ability to adapt.

1.3 From Command-And-Control to Trust-Based Autonomy

Prior to Agile, software projects were commonly managed through command-and-control structures such as the Waterfall model and its variants (Hoda et al., 2010). In these environments, roles were functionally siloed: analysts gathered requirements, developers wrote code and testers tested the code. The work was typically passed along a sequential pipeline. Managers controlled the planning, task allocation, and performance evaluation. Team members had little influence over decision-making or cross-functional collaboration.

This top-down model created distance between decision-makers and those performing the work. Trust was not a requirement; control mechanisms such as formal approvals, documentation, and rigid procedures substituted for interpersonal reliance. While this approach could maintain order, it often delayed response to change, stifled innovation, and hindered knowledge sharing.

Agile frameworks reimagine this structure entirely. Control is decentralised. Teams are expected to self-organise, define their own workflows, and collectively take ownership of outcomes. In this setting, trust must replace control. Team members need to believe that others will deliver what they commit to, raise blockers transparently, and support one another in achieving shared goals. Without this baseline trust, self-organisation breaks down, decision-making is delayed, and collaboration reverts to isolated individual effort.

As Moe and Dingsøyr (2008) argue, "Scrum is not very specific on how to establish mutual trust… although this is implicitly a prerequisite for a self-organizing team." In other words, Agile is built on the assumption of trust. However, *how* to build trust is never made explicit. This book seeks to address how trust can form.

1.4 Cognitive and Affective Trust: Dual Axes of Team Confidence

Trust in Agile teams is multi-dimensional. Two distinct types of trust are foundational in Agile teams:

- **Cognitive Trust** is built on belief in teammates' competence, reliability, and skill. In Scrum, credibility often comes from delivering on Sprint commitments consistently thus creating a predictable rhythm. The act of consistently following through on commitments plays a crucial role in building trust, not only among team members, but also in how the team is perceived by its stakeholders. When individuals deliver what they say they will, it reinforces reliability and strengthens the team's collective credibility (McAllister, 1995).
- **Affective Trust** is fostered through interpersonal warmth, shared goals, empathy, and mutual care. Agile's emphasis on short Sprints, Stand-ups, and Retrospectives encourages vulnerability and reinforces affective bonds. Admitting when help is needed is one of the most powerful behaviours for deepening trust as it signals honesty and authenticity, reduces psychological distance and invites reciprocity. Empirical studies suggest that affective trust, more than cognitive trust, strongly correlates with team performance (Webber, 2008).

These forms of trust support each other: cognitive trust enables initial cooperation, while affective trust fuels deeper collaboration and resilience.

1.5 Trust: The Backbone of Collaboration and Knowledge Sharing

In Agile software development, collaboration and knowledge sharing are not incidental activities but are integral to team success. Trust functions as an essential foundation upon which collaboration and knowledge sharing are built as opposed to being a desirable attribute in a team.

Within this paradigm, trust operates as a foundational element, enabling the interpersonal dynamics and information flows essential to delivering value during each Sprint. Trust is s a precondition for this to take place. When team members trust each other, they are more willing to share insights, challenge ideas constructively, and lean into the collective responsibility required by the Scrum framework.

The distinction between a group and a team is central to understanding how trust underpins collaboration. While a work group consists of individuals accountable only for their own contributions, a Scrum team is characterised by mutual accountability and shared goals. This structural difference fosters a context in which trust can flourish. The cross-functional composition of Scrum teams which brings together technical, design, and domain expertise, means that no one individual possesses all the answers. Trust in teammates' competence and reliability (cognitive trust) is therefore crucial. At the same time, affective trust which is based on interpersonal bonds, shared purpose, and emotional investment in outcomes, deepens commitment to collaborative effort.

Scrum rituals such as Sprint Planning, Daily Standups, and Retrospectives are designed to operationalise and sustain trust. These events facilitate transparency, visibility of progress, and frequent touchpoints for addressing blockers, all of which are critical to reinforcing team cohesion. Sprint Planning, for instance, not only aligns the team on objectives but also reinforces a shared mental model. When all members have visibility into who is doing what and why, trust in the process and in each other is strengthened.

The dual dimensions of trust, both cognitive and affective, also manifest in the way Scrum teams manage knowledge. Explicit knowledge, such as user stories, backlog items, and artefact documentation, is relatively easy to codify and share. Tacit knowledge, however, which can encompass know-how, system intuition, and contextual understanding, is far more difficult to communicate. Its transfer relies heavily on trust and proximity. When developers feel safe to ask questions, admit uncertainty, or offer alternative approaches, the team becomes a fertile ground for informal knowledge exchange. Pair programming, mentorship, and spontaneous conversations often become the vehicles for converting tacit knowledge into shared team insight.

Moreover, knowledge hoarding, which can be a significant impediment to team effectiveness, is less likely in a high-trust environment. When trust is low, individuals may guard information to preserve perceived status or control. When trust is high, team members are more likely to view knowledge as a collective asset, essential to shared success. In such environments, team members are also more open to being vulnerable i.e. by admitting when they need help or lack understanding. This vulnerability, when met with support rather than judgement, leads to learning, deeper competence, and stronger collaboration.

The shift from traditional command-and-control structures to self-organising teams in Agile further underscores the role of trust. In manager-led teams, decisions are made hierarchically, and control is externally imposed. In contrast, Scrum teams distribute decision-making authority internally. This decentralisation requires a high degree of mutual trust: in each other's capabilities, in each other's integrity, and in the team's shared objectives. It also requires role clarity, especially for the Product Owner, Scrum Master, and Development Team. This is so responsibilities are well understood, and potential ambiguities minimised. Such clarity creates a stable context within which trust can be built and maintained.

Trust becomes even more critical in distributed Scrum teams, where physical separation introduces new challenges to collaboration and cohesion. Without the benefit of co-location, the loss of shared physical context and spontaneous communication can erode team connectedness. In such settings, deliberate efforts are needed to maintain trust through regular communication, synchronised work rhythms, and intentional relationship-building practices.

In summary, trust serves as the connective tissue of collaboration and knowledge sharing in Agile teams. It enables individuals to move beyond task orientation toward collective ownership of outcomes. It transforms a set of contributors into a cohesive, high-performing team. Ultimately it lays the groundwork for continuous learning, innovation, and agility, qualities that are indispensable in today's complex software development landscape.

Agile thrives on ongoing teamwork, where developers openly exchange ideas and build solutions together. Daily stand-ups foster shared accountability, and meaningful collaboration flourishes only in environments which are grounded in mutual trust.

1.6 Swift Trust in Agile Teams

In many Agile environments, especially those that rely on time-boxed iterations like Sprints, individuals must collaborate immediately without the benefit of prolonged relationship-building. Rather than waiting for familiarity to develop over time, team members default to an assumption of competence, good intent, and reliability. This rapid development of trust is referred to as Swift Trust (Buvik, 2019).

This fast-tracked trust is underpinned by several features inherent to Scrum: role clarity, frequent interaction, and shared purpose. When roles such as Product Owner, Scrum Master, and Developer are well-defined, ambiguity is reduced, making it easier for individuals to trust that others will fulfil their responsibilities. Ceremonies such as the Daily Stand-up, Sprint Planning, and Sprint Reviews provide regular opportunities for open dialogue and transparent progress updates, which reinforce accountability and help team members confirm or adjust their initial assumptions about one another.

Swift trust is enabled by structural clarity but also by behavioural cues. For example, the importance of being able to ask for help cannot be over-emphasised as this is a marker of both humility and psychological safety. When team members admit they need assistance and are met with support rather than judgement, it fosters a virtuous cycle: help received enhances learning, which increases competence, and in turn reinforces trust (Edmondson & Mogelof, 2006). In this way, swift trust is converted into durable relational trust through repeated, affirming interactions.

Moreover, the willingness to show vulnerability and set aside ego plays a crucial role in the transition from swift to sustained trust. Teams that normalise help-seeking and collaborative problem-solving build deeper bonds and cultivate an atmosphere where knowledge is shared freely. In Agile environments where team compositions may shift frequently or deadlines are tight, this capacity for swift trust is a necessity.

However, the fragility of swift trust should not be overlooked. It must be actively nurtured through consistent behaviours, mutual respect, and frequent feedback loops. Without this, early assumptions may dissolve into suspicion or disengagement, especially under the pressures of delivery. Therefore, effective Scrum teams adopt rituals and norms that reinforce trust continuously, transforming initial faith into a robust culture of collaboration.

Swift trust allows Agile teams to move quickly from forming to performing. While it begins as an assumption, it becomes a reality through shared work, mutual accountability, and the deliberate cultivation of a supportive team ethos. In this sense, swift trust is not just a temporary bridge, it is a strategic enabler of high performance in Agile teams.

1.7 Trust Versus Traditional Controls

Traditional project management approaches, particularly those based on Waterfall or linear methodologies, rely heavily on formal controls such as detailed contracts, exhaustive documentation, and hierarchical oversight. These mechanisms are designed to minimise risk and enforce accountability by specifying expectations and deliverables in advance. In such models, trust is often subordinated to process, with compliance mechanisms acting as substitutes for collaborative alignment.

Agile methodologies offer a deliberate and radical departure from this paradigm. Instead of prescriptive control, Agile places trust at the centre of team dynamics and organisational functioning. The *Agile Manifesto* clearly reflects this shift by valuing "*individuals and interactions over processes and tools*" and "*customer collaboration over contract negotiation*" (Beck et al., 2001). Rather than treating trust as a peripheral cultural value, Agile treats it as a foundational operational principle that enables teams to function effectively in complex, fast-changing environments.

Trust in Agile contexts supports and sustains three interdependent dynamics: Collaboration, Adaptation, and Autonomy. High-trust environments facilitate open and honest communication, allowing teams to work together with clarity and psychological safety. Trust also enables adaptive capacity which allows teams to pivot, experiment, and refine solutions without the fear of blame or punitive scrutiny. Autonomy is likewise predicated on trust: Agile teams are expected to self-organise and make local decisions, a process that presupposes mutual confidence and shared accountability.

In contrast to traditional control mechanisms, which manage complexity through centralised planning and documentation, Agile teams manage complexity through iterative learning and decentralised decision-making. Trust reduces the need for micromanagement, shortens feedback loops, and fosters the kind of proactive behaviour that traditional models often suppress.

Moreover, Agile ceremonies such as Sprint Planning, Daily Stand-ups, and Retrospectives depend on and reinforce trust through transparency and mutual respect. When trust is lacking, these practices risk becoming performative or superficial, undermining their intended function.

Ultimately, as organisations adopt Agile principles, the locus of control shifts from formalised documentation and top-down governance to a trust-based model rooted in relational accountability. Trust thus becomes the structural scaffold that enables speed, innovation, and resilience, all qualities essential for success in uncertain and dynamic project environments.

1.8 Team Autonomy

Team autonomy is a foundational principle in Scrum. It is expressed through self-organisation and decentralised decision-making. Rather than adhering to hierarchical management or prescriptive control, Scrum empowers teams, particularly the Developers, to determine how best to accomplish their Sprint goals. This shift reflects a broader Agile ethos: the belief that those closest to the work are best positioned to make effective decisions, adapt quickly, and deliver value iteratively.

In practice, autonomy in Scrum means that teams assume ownership of planning, prioritisation, and process improvement in addition to execution (Mohagheghi et al., 2020). The Scrum framework provides the necessary scaffolding: roles, time-boxed events, and artefacts. Within this structure, teams operate with a high degree of independence. Autonomy, however, is not synonymous with a lack of coordination or accountability. It requires shared purpose, clarity, and above all, trust.

Trust is the enabling condition that allows team autonomy to function effectively. In high-trust environments, teams can communicate openly, make decisions collaboratively, and respond to challenges with agility rather than defensiveness. Trust reduces the need for external controls, enabling leaders to delegate authority with confidence and allowing team members to take the initiative without fear of blame. When trust is present, autonomy leads to innovation and adaptability; when it is absent, autonomy can quickly devolve into disconnection or risk aversion.

Moreover, trust activates and sustains the core Scrum values of focus, respect, openness, commitment and courage. When team members trust each other, they can focus fully on the Sprint without wasting energy on doubting their teammates. Trust fosters respect by encouraging the team members to value each other's skills and perspectives. It also enables openness as team members feel safe to voice concerns and admit mistakes they may have made. Commitment requires that team members invest fully in shared goals and deliverables; a process that is only sustainable when they trust one another to follow through. Courage, similarly, entails the willingness to take informed risks, challenge assumptions, and surface difficult truths during Sprint Reviews and Retrospectives. These behaviours demand psychological safety, which is inextricably linked to interpersonal and organisational trust.

Decentralised decision-making, which is a hallmark of Agile teams, depends on trust not only within the team but also between the team and stakeholders. Scrum ceremonies such as Sprint Planning, Daily Scrums, and Retrospectives are most effective when they occur in a climate of mutual respect and openness. Without trust, these events risk becoming procedural rather than transformational. Scrum events become mere rituals devoid of reflection or growth.

Ultimately, trust and autonomy are not independent attributes of effective Scrum teams; they are mutually reinforcing. Autonomy requires trust to avoid fragmentation, and trust finds expression through autonomous behaviour. Together, they form the cultural and operational bedrock of high-performing Agile teams, which are teams capable of delivering value consistently, adapting to change intelligently, and embodying the spirit of Scrum with integrity and resilience.

1.9 Trust as the Foundation of Sustainable Autonomy in Scrum

A central insight emerging from empirical studies of Scrum teams is that while autonomy is essential to Agile performance, it is only sustainable in environments characterised by high levels of trust. Scrum explicitly supports team autonomy through its structural emphasis on self-organisation, decentralised decision-making, and collective ownership of outcomes. However, these features do not operate in a vacuum. Autonomy that lacks a foundation of interpersonal and organisational trust quickly becomes unstable, leading to fragmentation, disengagement, or dysfunction.

Scrum teams are expected to self-organise: to determine internally how best to meet Sprint goals, distribute work, and respond to emerging challenges. This decentralised model assumes that team members can operate without micromanagement, make decisions close to the point of execution, and continuously improve their processes. However, these behaviours require a deep trust in one another's competence, intentions, and willingness to engage constructively. Without this relational trust, self-organisation deteriorates into siloed work or covert hierarchy, undermining the very agility Scrum is designed to support.

Trust serves not only as a social lubricant but also as an operational enabler. When trust is present, teams can exercise discretion with confidence, engage in open dialogue, and take ownership of both successes and failures. Trust facilitates the psychological safety necessary for creative risk-taking and honest reflection which are important conditions that underpin effective Sprint Reviews and Retrospectives. It also reduces reliance on formal controls and status reporting, allowing teams to focus on value creation rather than defensive justification.

Crucially, trust is also what activates and sustains key Scrum values, particularly commitment and courage. Commitment in Scrum requires individuals to dedicate themselves to shared goals and uphold mutual accountability. This level of engagement cannot be coerced; it must be freely given, and it emerges most reliably in high-trust environments. When team members believe that their contributions are respected and their efforts supported, they are more likely to commit fully to the team's objectives and uphold its delivery standards.

Similarly, courage, which can be thought of as the willingness to confront uncertainty, challenge ideas, and address difficult issues, relies on a foundation of trust. Team members must feel safe to take interpersonal and technical risks, whether by questioning scope, experimenting with new approaches, or surfacing blockers. In low-trust environments, such behaviours are rare, as individuals often prioritise self-preservation over constructive engagement. In contrast, high-trust teams exhibit the psychological safety and moral strength required to enact Scrum's most demanding principles.

In summary, while Scrum provides the scaffolding for team autonomy, it is trust that fills that structure with purpose and resilience. Autonomy without trust leads to inconsistency and withdrawal; trust without autonomy becomes passivity. When the two operate in tandem, however, they enable Scrum teams to act with confidence, commit to outcomes, and face challenges with courage, characteristics of authentic and high-performing Agile practice.

1.10 Operationalising Team Autonomy in Scrum

Team autonomy is a core tenet of Scrum, representing the ability of teams to self-organise, make independent decisions about how to approach their work, and assume collective responsibility for outcomes. This autonomy enables responsiveness, innovation, and continuous improvement all of which are hallmarks of Agile practice. Autonomy is not characterised by the absence of structure, instead it is implemented by a redistribution of control from centralised management to the team itself.

In Scrum, autonomy begins with the understanding that teams determine *how* to accomplish the goals agreed upon during Sprint Planning. Once the Product Owner sets the *what* i.e. the priorities and intended value, the Development Team is empowered to make all decisions regarding execution. This includes defining tasks, setting the internal workflow, resolving dependencies, and adapting approaches throughout the Sprint. This freedom to choose how work is executed fosters ownership, engagement, and efficiency.

A key feature of Scrum autonomy is the collective responsibility for the Sprint Goal. In addition to completing a set of backlog items, the team commits to achieving a cohesive outcome that delivers value. This shared commitment creates a sense of mutual accountability, encouraging collaboration and reinforcing the idea that success or failure is owned by the team as a whole, not by individuals acting in isolation.

Autonomy is further embedded in Scrum through its role definitions. The Development Team operates without a project manager directing day-to-day work. Instead, the team is expected to organise itself, decide how best to complete the work, and make adjustments based on feedback and context. The Scrum Master facilitates this process but does not interfere with any of the technical decisions. Likewise, the Product Owner sets priorities and ensures alignment with stakeholder needs but does not dictate how the team should implement those priorities.

This deliberate separation of concerns ensures that decision-making authority resides where the technical expertise and situational awareness exist i.e. within the team. It also reduces dependency on hierarchical structures, shortens feedback loops, and promotes agility in the face of change.

However, such autonomy depends on a foundation of trust. Teams must trust one another to follow through on commitments, raise issues transparently, and act in the collective interest. Similarly, stakeholders and organisational leaders must trust the team's capacity to deliver, rather than attempting to control outcomes through top-down directives. Without this mutual trust, autonomy can degrade into misalignment, risk aversion, or superficial engagement.

Ultimately, team autonomy in Scrum is operationalised through decentralised decision-making, shared ownership of goals, and structural support via clearly defined roles. When combined with trust and a culture of accountability, autonomy becomes a powerful driver of agility, empowering teams to deliver value consistently and adapt effectively in complex, evolving environments.

1.11 Trust as the Enabler of Autonomy

While autonomy is a structural feature of Scrum, its practical sustainability is contingent on trust. Trust acts as the enabling condition that allows autonomy to be exercised meaningfully, rather than performed superficially. Without trust, team autonomy can falter, manifesting as either cautious disengagement or fragmented self-direction. With trust, however, autonomy becomes a driver of creativity, cohesion, and accountability.

Research reveals that trust is deeply interwoven with psychological safety (O'Connell & Molloy, 2019). Another reinforcing construct is distributed leadership. Autonomy in Scrum presupposes that decision-making is decentralised i.e. that leadership is not confined to formal authority but is instead distributed across the team. This model of leadership demands mutual confidence in one another's capabilities, intentions, and judgment. Teams can only function with this level of distributed responsibility if trust is present both laterally (among peers) and vertically (with stakeholders and leadership).

In high-trust environments, individuals step into leadership roles fluidly based on expertise, context, or initiative. They do so because the culture permits and supports such contribution. Trust in this context is functional as opposed to relational. It enables responsiveness by allowing those closest to the work to make decisions without fear of reprimand or the need for excessive justification.

Equally critical is the role of trust in creating and maintaining psychological safety which is the shared belief that the team is a safe space for interpersonal risk-taking. Trust and psychological safety are mutually reinforcing i.e. trust encourages openness, and openness deepens trust. In the absence of trust, team members may withhold dissenting views, avoid asking for help, or suppress uncertainties. These are behaviours that erode autonomy and lead to compliance rather than contribution. By contrast, where trust is strong, teams can engage in the kinds of difficult, exploratory, or corrective conversations that are essential to continuous improvement.

Autonomy, rather than being a structural condition enabled by the Scrum framework, is a behavioural and relational dynamic. Trust allows leaders to step back without abdicating responsibility, and it allows team members to step forward without hesitation. Teams that trust each other work with greater fluidity, make faster decisions, and exhibit stronger alignment around shared goals.

Furthermore, open communication has been identified as a core behaviour in successful teams. It is both a product of trust and a mechanism for reinforcing it. When trust exists, teams share knowledge proactively, voice concerns early, and invite feedback freely. These practices, in turn, reinforce the team's collective autonomy by enabling adaptive coordination and emergent decision-making.

In summary, trust enables autonomy by activating internal leadership, mutual support, and psychological resilience. Where trust is present, autonomy in Scrum teams leads to genuine self-organisation, faster feedback cycles, and stronger ownership of outcomes. Where trust is lacking, autonomy collapses into either passivity or chaos. Thus, cultivating trust is not ancillary to Agile practice, it is foundational.

1.12 Shared Decision-Making and Collective Accountability

In Scrum, effective team performance relies on technical competence but also on the relational and procedural conditions that allow teams to make decisions together and own their outcomes collectively. These conditions are most robust in high-trust environments, where mutual respect, transparency, and psychological safety are present. In such settings, shared decision-making and collective accountability emerge as everyday operational practices, not just as aspirational ideals.

Trust enables open negotiation of work during Sprint Planning, where team members collaboratively and collectively determine what can be accomplished in the upcoming Sprint and how best to approach it. Rather than receiving directives, teams in high-trust environments engage in meaningful dialogue with the Product Owner to clarify scope, negotiate commitments, and calibrate capacity. This process reflects a mutual understanding that decision-making authority is shared and that every voice carries weight. Trust allows for honest assessments of feasibility, open discussions about constraints, and constructive pushback, when necessary, all of which lead to stronger alignment and more realistic planning.

During the Sprint itself, real-time decisions can be made without the need for hierarchical escalation. When trust is strong, team members feel empowered to act decisively in the face of uncertainty, adapting plans or reconfiguring tasks as new information emerges. This autonomy reduces dependency on external approvals and enables faster response times which is an essential capability in Agile contexts. It also reinforces distributed leadership, as team members confidently rely on each other's expertise and judgment to move work forward.

Trust is equally vital in Sprint Retrospectives, where the focus shifts to reflection, learning, and continuous improvement. In low-trust teams, retrospectives risk becoming ritualistic or evasive, with team members reluctant to surface difficult issues or admit mistakes. In contrast, high-trust teams use Retrospectives as safe spaces for honest dialogue, where successes are acknowledged, failures are analysed without blame, and process adjustments are made collaboratively. This reflective practice is only effective when team members believe they can speak candidly without fear of judgment or retaliation. This is a belief rooted in psychological safety and reinforced by consistent, trust-based interactions.

Together, these practices illustrate how shared decision-making and collective accountability are outcomes of a trust-rich environment. In such contexts, team members are responsible not only for individual tasks but for the success of the whole. They hold each other accountable, share risks and rewards, and contribute to the continuous evolution of team performance.

Ultimately, trust acts as both the precondition and product of shared decision-making and collective accountability. It enables teams to plan with clarity, act with autonomy, and reflect with honesty. These behaviours, when sustained, create a resilient team culture capable of learning, adapting, and delivering value at a consistently high level.

1.13 Collective Ownership and Shared Decision-Making

A defining feature of effective Scrum teams is the shift from individual task ownership to collective ownership of goals. In high-trust environments, decision-making is a shared endeavour, grounded in transparency, psychological safety, and mutual accountability. These conditions allow teams to operate as cohesive units as opposed to loose collections of individuals performing assigned tasks.

During Sprint Planning, shared decision-making becomes particularly visible. Instead of passively accepting a prescribed workload, team members actively negotiate the scope of the Sprint based on realistic capacity, technical complexity, and evolving product priorities. This process is enabled by a trust-based culture in which team members can speak candidly, challenge assumptions, and calibrate commitments without fear of blame or scrutiny. The result is a more realistic plan but also a plan that is collectively owned and understood.

This sense of ownership carries forward into the execution of the Sprint. In high-trust teams, real-time decisions about how to adjust, re-prioritise, or reallocate work do not require escalation. Instead, the team collaboratively makes context-sensitive decisions as new information emerges. These autonomous adjustments reflect a deep alignment around shared goals, as well as confidence in one another's judgment and integrity. Distributed leadership naturally emerges in such contexts, with individuals stepping into leadership roles as needed based on their expertise and situational awareness.

The Sprint Retrospective further reinforces collective ownership. Teams with strong relational trust use retrospectives as spaces for shared reflection and constructive critique. In these settings, challenges are framed as team issues rather than individual failures, and solutions are co-created. This behavioural pattern is sustained by psychological safety, which allows team members to engage in difficult conversations and take responsibility for both outcomes and process improvements.

Collective ownership, then, is a behavioural norm reinforced through trust. When trust is present, team members orient themselves towards team-level outcomes, and they hold one another accountable in ways that are supportive rather than punitive. The emphasis moves away from solely completing just their own tasks. This cultural shift enables greater agility, resilience, and adaptability, qualities which are essential for high-performing Scrum teams.

1.14 Connection to Scrum Values

The Scrum values: Commitment, Courage, Focus, Openness, and Respect, serve as behavioural cornerstones for Agile teams. Among these, *commitment* and *courage* are particularly dependent on the presence of interpersonal and organisational trust. While these values are often stated as aspirational norms, their consistent enactment in practice is only possible when the emotional and psychological conditions that sustain them are intentionally supported. Trust is the foundation upon which these conditions are built.

In high-trust environments, commitment to Sprint goals is far more than a contractual agreement; it is a collective investment in a shared outcome. Teams that trust one another and their stakeholders are more likely to engage sincerely in planning activities, negotiate goals transparently, and follow through with integrity. This form of commitment is grounded in mutual support where team members know they can rely on one another, raise difficulties without fear, and collaborate under pressure. Trust transforms commitment from obligation to ownership, enhancing both motivation and accountability.

Equally, courage in Scrum involves the willingness to act, but also the capacity to challenge assumptions, voice concerns, and experiment with uncertainty. Trust empowers individuals to take interpersonal and technical risks without fear of ridicule, rejection, or retaliation. Teams that lack trust often avoid hard conversations, conceal doubts, or disengage from retrospective feedback, all of which undermine the continuous improvement ethos at the heart of Scrum. Conversely, teams that operate in a climate of trust can speak candidly, propose bold solutions, and confront failure constructively.

The connection between trust and these values is reinforced by the concept of psychological safety, which has been shown to be a key enabler of open communication and adaptive behaviour. Psychological safety allows team members to admit mistakes, seek help, or offer dissenting opinions, all of which require courage. It also supports commitment by reinforcing that contributions are valued and that challenges will be met with collaboration, not criticism. In this way, trust does not merely support the functional aspects of Scrum, it sustains its ethical and relational integrity.

Without trust, commitment risks becoming performative as teams may agree to Sprint goals but withhold full engagement. Similarly, courage may be suppressed by fear of exposure or exclusion, particularly in teams where past experiences of judgement or micromanagement remain unresolved. These dysfunctional patterns directly contradict the spirit of Scrum and limit a team's capacity to improve and innovate.

Overall, trust is a prerequisite for authentic alignment with the Scrum values. It creates the psychological conditions under which these values are not only expressed but lived. Where trust is strong, these values become embedded in daily interactions and team rituals. Where trust is weak, they remain abstract ideals; frequently visible in documentation but absent in practice.

1.15 Consequences of Low-Trust Environments

While high-trust environments enable autonomy, collaboration, and accountability, low-trust environments introduce significant constraints on team functioning and, ultimately, on the effectiveness of Scrum itself. Trust is an operational necessity not an interpersonal nicety. Without it, the foundational elements of Scrum: self-organisation, empirical process control, and team-based ownership, begin to break down.

In low-trust teams, autonomy becomes source of risk as opposed to a strength. Team members may perceive self-organisation as abandonment rather than empowerment, leading to guarded behaviour, indecision, or excessive reliance on external validation. In such environments, autonomy often becomes superficial i.e. formally encouraged but practically avoided, as team members lack the psychological safety required to make and own meaningful decisions.

This erosion of trust affects behaviour in measurable ways. Ideas are withheld, not because they lack merit, but because individuals fear judgement or reprisals. Deference to hierarchy resurfaces, even in flat or self-managing structures, as team members seek protection from blame rather than pursuing collaborative problem-solving. Ownership is diluted, with individuals focusing on assigned tasks rather than collective goals, weakening both cohesion and accountability.

Such dynamics undermine the integrity of Scrum implementation. Without trust, Scrum roles lose their functional clarity. The Product Owner may be viewed with suspicion rather than as a partner in delivering value to the customer. The Scrum Master's facilitative role may be misinterpreted as managerial oversight, reintroducing control in disguised forms. The Development Team may default to passive execution rather than active ownership, compromising self-organisation. These patterns often lead to what is commonly referred to as "*cargo cult*" agility, where Scrum rituals are followed mechanically, but the underlying values and principles are absent.

In these scenarios, Sprint Planning becomes performative, with unrealistic commitments made to appease stakeholders. Daily Scrums devolve into status updates rather than opportunities for coordination. Retrospectives are treated as procedural obligations, lacking the openness required for genuine reflection or process improvement. This superficial imitation of Agile practices not only limits team growth but can also reinforce cynicism about Agile itself, leading organisations to conclude that Scrum "doesn't work," when, in reality, the failure lies in the absence of trust. In contrast, high-trust environments support adaptive behaviour, shared leadership, and continuous learning, all of which are essential to the spirit and success of Scrum. The contrast between these two contexts illustrates that trust is not an intangible contributor to be assumed, but a necessary structural component to be cultivated. Its absence reshapes team culture, disables Scrum's mechanisms, and ultimately constrains the very agility organisations seek to achieve.

1.16 Concluding Remarks

This chapter has demonstrated that trust is not a peripheral or abstract concept in Agile practice. It is the foundation upon which effective Scrum teams are built and sustained. Beginning with the shift from command-and-control models to trust-based autonomy, this chapter has explored how trust enables decentralised decision-making, supports collective ownership of outcomes, and underpins psychological safety. The dual dimensions of cognitive and affective trust, were briefly examined, showing how both are essential to fostering collaboration, knowledge sharing, and resilience in Agile environments. Furthermore, the chapter highlighted how trust activates core Scrum values such as focus, respect, openness, commitment and courage, allowing teams to move beyond procedural compliance toward authentic engagement.

The consequences of low-trust environments were also made clear: superficial autonomy, withheld insights, role confusion, and performative agility that undermines the very principles Scrum aims to uphold. In contrast, high-trust cultures create conditions for distributed leadership, real-time adaptation, and reflective learning. These are outcomes that are critical in today's volatile, complex, and fast-paced software development contexts.

Strategically, this reframes trust from a cultural "nice-to-have" into an organisational imperative. For Agile leaders, this means shifting attention from process fidelity to relational health. Trust must be cultivated intentionally. This can be achieved through role clarity, psychological safety, vulnerability-based leadership, and consistent reinforcement of shared norms. Organisations seeking to scale Agile must embed trust-building into onboarding, team formation, feedback mechanisms, and leadership development, recognising that the speed and quality of delivery depend less on tools or artefacts and more on the relational infrastructure of the team.

In essence, trust is not just the condition that allows Agile to function. It is the catalyst that enables teams to thrive. It shapes how people collaborate, learn, and lead. Agile success, therefore, is not simply about executing frameworks but about sustaining the trust that makes those frameworks meaningful. As such, the real measure of agility may be less about velocity or burn-down charts and more about the quality of trust that holds the team together in the face of complexity and change.

References

Beck, K., Beedle, M., Van Bennekum, A., Cockburn, A., Cunningham, W., Fowler, M., ... & Thomas, D. (2001). Manifesto for agile software development.

Buvik, M. P. (2019). The significance of trust in project teams: Exploring context-dependent antecedents and consequences of trust in a project team setting.

Edmondson, A. C., & Mogelof, J. P. (2006). Explaining psychological safety in innovation teams: organizational culture, team dynamics, or personality? In *Creativity and innovation in organizational teams* (pp. 129–156). Psychology Press.

Hoda, R., Noble, J., & Marshall, S. (2010, May). Organizing self-organizing teams. In *Proceedings of the 32nd ACM/IEEE International Conference on Software Engineering-Volume 1* (pp. 285–294).

McAllister, D. J. (1995). Affect-and cognition-based trust as foundations for interpersonal cooperation in organizations. *Academy of Management Journal, 38*(1), 24–59.

Moe, N. B., & Dingsøyr, T. (2008). Scrum and team effectiveness: Theory and practice. In P. Abrahamsson, R. Baskerville, K. Conboy, B. Fitzgerald, L. Morgan, & X. Wang (eds.), *Agile Processes in Software Engineering and Extreme Programming.* XP 2008. Lecture Notes in Business Information Processing, vol 9. Springer. https://doi.org/10.1007/978-3-540-68255-4_2

Mohagheghi, P., Lassenius, C., & Bakken, I. O. (2020, June). Enabling team autonomy in a large public organization. In *International Conference on Agile Software Development* (pp. 245–252). Springer International Publishing.

O'Connell, T., & Molloy, O. (2019). Trust: Promoting interdependence, knowledge sharing & collaboration in scrum teams. In *Proceedings of the International Conference on Software Engineering Research and Practice (SERP)* (pp. 10–18). The Steering Committee of The World Congress in Computer Science, Computer Engineering and Applied Computing (WorldComp).

Webber, S. S. (2008). Development of cognitive and affective trust in teams: A longitudinal study. *Small Group Research, 39*(6), 746–769.

Chapter 2
The Science of Trust

Abstract Trust is the cornerstone of effective collaboration, shaping how individuals share knowledge, navigate uncertainty, and work toward shared goals. This chapter explores trust as a dynamic, multi-layered construct, spanning cognitive, affective, emotional, social, and psychological dimensions. Drawing on long-standing but timeless frameworks, it distinguishes between cognitive trust, built on competence and reliability, and affective trust, rooted in empathy and emotional connection. Focusing on Agile environments, particularly Scrum teams, the chapter examines how trust supports psychological safety, shared decision-making, and high performance in both co-located and distributed settings. It addresses common barriers to trust, including hierarchy, miscommunication, and past breaches, and presents enablers such as open dialogue, leadership vulnerability, and collective purpose. Trust is presented as something that must be built, maintained, and nurtured over time. Far from being a soft value, trust is shown to be a critical enabler of creativity, adaptability, and cohesion in complex, collaborative work.

2.1 Introduction

Trust is a cornerstone of effective collaboration, whether in intimate personal relationships, organisational teams, or complex societal systems. It shapes how individuals engage with one another, share knowledge, and navigate uncertainty. Trust fosters cooperation which reduces the need for constant oversight and enables adaptive problem-solving in dynamic environments. Yet, trust is far from a simple or static construct. It evolves through interactions, balancing rational assessments of competence and integrity with emotional bonds and shared experiences.

This chapter explores the science of trust, dissecting its two primary forms: *cognitive trust*, grounded in rational judgment and predictability, and *affective trust*, which arises from emotional connections and shared values. By understanding these dimensions, Agile teams can better appreciate how trust underpins effective collaboration, whether in local co-located Scrum teams or distributed Agile settings.

T. O'Connell, *Trust in Agile Teams*,
SpringerBriefs in Computer Science, https://doi.org/10.1007/978-3-032-21963-3_2

This chapter draws upon foundational theories of trust (e.g., Mayer et al., 1995; McAllister, 1995), which, despite their age, remain widely cited and continue to shape our contemporary understanding of trust in collaborative contexts. Alongside empirical research and practical frameworks, notably McKnight and Chervany's (1996) typology of trust, these models offer a robust conceptual foundation for examining how trust underpins collaborative engagement, facilitates knowledge sharing, and functions in practice. While the focus is predominantly on Agile software development, the discussion extends more broadly to the dynamics of trust across diverse team-based environments.

2.2 Cognitive Trust: The Calculus of Collaboration

Cognitive trust arises from rational evaluations of a colleague's competence, reliability, and integrity. It is built upon evidence including observed behaviour, consistency, past performance, and reputation (Mayer et al., 1995; McAllister, 1995). This form of trust aligns with the definition of trust as "the willingness of a party to be vulnerable to the actions of another party based on the expectation that the other will perform a particular action important to the trustor, irrespective of the ability to monitor or control that other party" (Mayer et al., 1995, p. 712).

In team settings, cognitive trust forms the scaffolding for collaboration. Individuals rely on demonstrated competence in technical skills, problem-solving, or decision-making. This early-stage trust, often termed *calculus-based trust*, is transactional and rooted in self-interest (Lewicki & Bunker, 1995). It arises from a weighing of the costs and benefits of trusting another, where compliance is driven more by deterrence or reputation than by intrinsic motivation.

Without cognitive trust, the open exchange of critical information is hampered. High cognitive trust facilitates the flow of relevant, accurate, and comprehensive information, contributing to better decision-making and problem-solving (Zand, 1972). Conversely, low cognitive trust can result in information withholding, reduced influence, and stifled innovation. Trust, in this sense, can be seen as a calculated decision influenced by risk and expected outcomes (Shapiro et al., 1992).

Cognitive trust evolves through iterative stages, transitioning from calculus-based trust to *knowledge-based trust*, where predictability and consistent behaviour foster a more stable collaborative environment (Lewicki & Bunker, 1995). This progression can be mapped onto McKnight and Chervany's (1996) typology which incorporates trusting beliefs, intentions, and behaviours (cf, Sect. 2.7). Together these scaffold effective collaboration.

2.3 Affective Trust: The Glue of Social Bonds

In contrast to the rationality of cognitive trust, affective trust emerges from emotional bonds, shared experiences, and mutual care. It is grounded in reciprocated interpersonal concern, empathy, and benevolence (McAllister, 1995). This form of trust evolves as team members demonstrate empathy, engage in discretionary behaviours supporting others, and invest emotionally in their relationships.

The ambiguity in human relationships underscores affective trust, where trust bridges the gap between knowledge and uncertainty, embodying confidence in probable outcomes despite incomplete information (Simmel, 1950). Affective trust often requires a leap of faith: a belief in a colleague's goodwill and care beyond task-based interactions.

Research suggests that a foundation of cognitive trust is often necessary for affective trust to develop (McAllister, 1995). Initial reliance on competence and reliability creates conditions for deeper emotional bonds. This evolution mirrors models that describe trust progressing through stages: predictability, dependability, and ultimately faith (Rempel et al., 1985).

Affective trust is also associated with benevolence, the belief that a colleague genuinely cares about one's welfare beyond self-interest (Mayer et al., 1995). This dimension is reflected in behaviours such as offering help, sharing emotional support, and fostering a culture of psychological safety.

Strong interpersonal ties, characterized by high emotional intensity, intimacy, and reciprocal support, form the bedrock of affective trust in teams (Granovetter, 1973, 1983). Such ties emerge over time, rooted in shared experiences and sustained interaction (Barbalet, 1996; Khodyakov, 2007).

2.4 The Emotional Aspect of Trust

Rather than being merely a rational calculation of risks and rewards, trust also has a distinctly emotional dimension that powerfully shapes collaborative behaviour. This emotional aspect is especially critical in team settings, where members routinely navigate uncertainty, interdependence, and shared goals.

When trust is low, people often conceal or distort information to protect themselves, leading to communication that is less accurate, less comprehensive, and less timely. This defensive stance limits collective problem-solving because individuals fear exposure or blame. Mistrust also generates a feedback loop of suspicion and guardedness, as team members reject influence from one another, resist coordination, and minimise interdependence.

By contrast, high-trust environments encourage open, candid exchanges. When people trust each other, they share information freely, and they do this even when it exposes their own uncertainties or mistakes. This vulnerability enables others to influence their thinking and jointly refine ideas. Trust reduces social uncertainty, increases psychological safety, and creates the conditions for realistic, creative, and long-range solutions to emerge.

At its core, the emotional aspect of trust supports a climate of shared vulnerability. When team members feel secure enough to admit errors, seek help, or challenge assumptions, they strengthen collective learning and adaptability. This emotional foundation is essential to unlocking the full collaborative potential of trust.

2.5 The Social Dimension of Trust

While trust operates at the level of individual beliefs and emotions, it is also fundamentally a social phenomenon embedded in relationships and networks. Interpersonal ties vary in their strength, shaped by factors such as time spent together, emotional intensity, mutual confiding, and reciprocal support. These strong ties form the basis for high levels of trust within teams.

Strong ties typically develop through repeated interaction and shared experiences. They promote motivation to assist one another and offer reliable channels for confidential or sensitive information exchange. This creates a stable foundation for cooperation, particularly in environments marked by complexity or uncertainty. Conversely, weak ties, involving connections that are less emotionally intense and less frequent, often provide access to novel information and external perspectives, making them valuable for innovation and boundary-spanning.

Trust also functions as a collective property of teams and organisations. It emerges from shared expectations about reliable, reciprocal behaviour, and is reinforced by group norms and cultural values. In diverse or cross-functional teams, building trust requires navigating different expectations, communication styles, and cultural assumptions. Recognising trust as a socially constructed and context-dependent process allows teams to intentionally cultivate norms that support transparency, accountability, and mutual respect.

Ultimately, trust is a social practice shaped by the broader network of relationships and institutional contexts in which collaboration unfolds. In this sense it is more than a personal decision.

2.6 Psychological Models of Trust

In addition to its rational, emotional, and social facets, trust can be understood as a deeply psychological process. Psychological models of trust highlight how individual dispositions, perceptions of others, and interpersonal experiences shape one's willingness to rely on others despite uncertainty or risk.

For example, some individuals have a generalised propensity to trust others based on past experiences or personality traits. This dispositional trust influences how quickly and easily they extend trust in new relationships. Beyond this baseline inclination, psychological theories emphasise the role of expectations and motivations in trust development. Trust often rests on beliefs about a partner's ability, integrity, and benevolence, which together shape the decision to become vulnerable to another's actions.

Trust also evolves through repeated interactions that test and refine these expectations. Early stages may involve cautious, calculated exchanges aimed at verifying predictability. Over time, relationships can deepen into more personal, *identification-based trust*, where partners internalise one another's goals and act with mutual understanding and care (Lewicki & Wiethoff, 2000).

Furthermore, psychological models underscore that trust shapes not only what individuals expect of others but also how they interpret others' behaviour. High levels of trust lead to more generous interpretations of ambiguous actions and reduce the perceived need for monitoring and control. This interpretive lens becomes especially important in collaborative settings, where misaligned expectations can quickly erode cooperation.

By acknowledging trust as a psychological phenomenon, teams can better appreciate the individual differences, motivations, and perceptions that affect collective performance. This perspective reinforces the need for deliberate, reflective practices that nurture trust as a dynamic, evolving relationship as opposed to a static condition.

2.7 The Interplay of Cognitive and Affective Trust

Cognitive and affective trust are conceptually distinct yet deeply interconnected. While cognitive trust often lays the groundwork through assessments of competence and reliability, affective trust emerges through shared experiences, benevolence, and emotional resonance. Their relationship is complementary and sequential, evolving as teams deepen their collaborative engagement.

A key element underpinning both forms of trust is vulnerability which is the willingness to be exposed to risk in the expectation of positive outcomes. Cognitive trust involves measured vulnerability, where evidence of competence justifies reliance. Affective trust, however, requires deeper, more personal vulnerability, encompassing care, loyalty, and mutual support (Mishra, 1996). This vulnerability fosters psychological safety, creating a space where individuals feel safe to admit mistakes, seek help, and express concerns.

McKnight and Chervany's (1996) framework offers a nuanced lens for understanding trust in collaborative contexts. Their typology conceptualises trust as an interrelated system which encompasses an individual's disposition to trust (aligned with cognitive trust), the institutional conditions that enable or constrain trust, the trusting intentions or willingness of the individual to accept vulnerability (bridging cognitive and affective trust), and the enactment of trust through trusting behaviours (manifesting trust through actions). Dispositional trust and situational decisions to trust further moderate these dynamics, shaping how individuals interpret evidence and determine their willingness to trust.

2.8 Theoretical Models in the Trust Domain

While much of this chapter has focused on conceptual foundations of trust, including cognitive, affective, and social dimensions, there is also a body of research that examines how trust functions specifically within team contexts.

Although there is no published research that deals with trust in Scrum teams per se, several scholars have explored trust in teamwork and its impact on team effectiveness more broadly.

Costa (2003) investigated trust in work teams, concluding that it is best understood as a *multi-component construct* that influences performance. She identified the importance of both cognitive and affective elements in building and sustaining trust over time.

Salas et al. (2005) conducted an extensive review of the teamwork literature, distilling findings into what they termed the "Big Five" of teamwork: team leadership, mutual performance monitoring, backup behaviour, adaptability, and team orientation. They also highlighted coordinating mechanisms, including trust, that underpin effective teamwork.

More recently, Costa et al. (2018) have reviewed theoretical and empirical literature on *trust emergence and development in teams*, examining the dynamic, context-dependent processes through which trust evolves in collaborative settings.

These models illustrate that trust in teams is complex and multi-dimensional, reinforcing the importance of understanding its cognitive, affective, and social foundations. They also provide useful frameworks for analysing trust in Agile and Scrum teams, offering insights into how trust develops, sustains team cohesion, and enables effective collaboration in fast-paced, iterative environments.

2.9 Barriers and Enablers of Trust

While trust is critical to effective collaboration, it does not arise automatically or uniformly across contexts. Teams must navigate a range of factors that can either enable or inhibit trust-building processes.

Barriers to trust often stem from power dynamics, organisational structures, or cultural misalignments. Hierarchical legacies can discourage open communication, as individuals may fear judgement or reprisal when sharing uncertainty or challenging ideas. Differences in cultural norms and communication styles can also lead to misinterpretations of intent, eroding confidence and creating suspicion. Past breaches of trust, such as broken commitments or inconsistent behaviour, can leave lasting scepticism that inhibits future cooperation.

Trust is also undermined by practices that prioritise monitoring and control over autonomy. Excessive reliance on formal contracts, rigid rules, or punitive oversight can signal a lack of faith in team members' intentions or competence, fostering defensive behaviour and information hoarding. Once established, patterns of mistrust can become self-reinforcing cycles in which suspicion leads to concealment, which then confirms the original doubts.

Enablers of trust, by contrast, involve intentional efforts to reduce perceived risks and build shared understanding. Psychological safety is one of the most important enablers, providing a climate where individuals feel secure enough to admit mistakes, ask questions, and seek help without fear of negative consequences. Regular, transparent communication helps align expectations, clarify goals, and surface potential misunderstandings early.

Shared goals and interdependence also motivate trustworthy behaviour, as individuals recognise their success depends on collective outcomes. Leadership behaviours that model vulnerability, such as acknowledging uncertainty or seeking feedback, can further normalise openness and encourage reciprocity. Over time, repeated positive interactions reinforce trust, transforming initial cautious agreements into deeper, more resilient relationships.

Recognising these barriers and enablers allows teams and organisations to cultivate trust intentionally rather than leaving it to chance. By designing structures, practices, and cultures that support transparency, accountability, and mutual respect, the conditions necessary for effective, adaptive collaboration can be created. Structures such as clearly defined roles (e.g., Product Owner, Scrum Master, Developers), team charters, and visible work boards help reduce ambiguity and foster shared understanding. Practices like Daily Stand-ups, Sprint Reviews, and Retrospectives promote regular communication, continuous improvement, and honest reflection. Incorporating peer feedback mechanisms and blameless post-mortems further strengthens psychological safety and collective accountability. Culturally, high-trust environments are reinforced by leaders who model vulnerability, encourage inclusive decision-making, and treat respectful dissent as a valuable contribution rather than a disruption. Celebrating learning, especially from failure, signals that growth and innovation are valued over perfection. Together, these elements form the relational and operational backbone of teams capable of navigating complexity with resilience, cohesion, and sustained trust.

2.10 Concluding Remarks

Trust is not just a simple prerequisite for collaboration; it is the essential fabric that holds collaborative efforts together, allowing people to work toward shared goals in the face of uncertainty and complexity. As this chapter has shown, trust is not a monolithic or static construct but a dynamic, evolving phenomenon shaped by rational judgments, emotional bonds, social contexts, and psychological processes.

Cognitive trust provides the foundational scaffolding for effective teamwork. Built on perceptions of competence, reliability, and integrity, it enables team members to take calculated risks, share critical information, and align their efforts toward common objectives. This form of trust supports the efficient exchange of knowledge and reduces the need for burdensome oversight, laying the groundwork for coordinated action even in complex, high-stakes environments.

However, collaboration cannot thrive on rational calculation alone. Affective trust deepens these relationships through emotional bonds forged in empathy, mutual care, and shared experience. It requires individuals to go beyond transactional exchanges, embracing vulnerability and demonstrating a willingness to support one another, even when doing so carries personal risk. This trust nurtures psychological safety, creating an environment where people feel secure enough to admit mistakes, seek help, challenge assumptions, and engage in honest, creative dialogue.

The emotional and social dimensions of trust further underscore its complexity. Trust is a relational practice embedded in networks of strong and weak ties. Strong interpersonal connections develop through sustained interaction, shared goals, and reciprocal support, fostering a resilient sense of loyalty and obligation. Meanwhile, weak ties can introduce fresh ideas and expand access to new resources, illustrating that trust is both inwardly cohesive and outwardly adaptive.

Psychological models serve to remind us that trust is deeply personal. Individuals bring their own histories, predispositions, and interpretive lenses to every interaction, shaping how they perceive others' intentions and decide when to become vulnerable. This variability demands sensitivity to individual differences, motivations, and past experiences when designing collaborative practices.

However, understanding the forms and dynamics of trust is only half the story. Teams and organisations must also recognise the barriers that routinely undermine trust. Hierarchical structures, rigid control systems, and punitive cultures can create climates of fear, which foster defensive behaviours and discourage open communication. Cultural differences in norms and communication styles can lead to misinterpretations, suspicion, and unintended conflict. Past breaches of trust can leave a lasting residue of scepticism that undermines and may eliminate future cooperation.

Conversely, trust can be intentionally cultivated through deliberate enablers. Psychological safety stands out as a vital condition, allowing people to speak freely without fear of reprisal or ridicule. Leadership that models vulnerability i.e. admitting uncertainty, inviting feedback, and acknowledging mistakes, sets a powerful example that normalises openness and reciprocity. Shared goals and interdependence motivate trustworthy behaviour, as team members recognise their success depends on collective achievement. Transparent communication, consistent follow-through, and repeated positive interactions build trust incrementally, transforming initial caution into deep, resilient collaboration.

Ultimately, trust is a living process that requires ongoing care and commitment. It is shaped by context, sustained by practices, and reinforced through shared successes and failures. In collaborative work, trust is what transforms a collection of skilled individuals into a cohesive, adaptive team capable of navigating complexity and uncertainty with confidence and creativity.

By mapping these diverse dimensions, cognitive and affective, emotional and social, psychological, and organisational, onto frameworks like McKnight and Chervany's typology this chapter provides a conceptual toolkit for understanding trust in all its richness. This foundation prepares us to move beyond theory into practice.

Chapter 3 will build on these insights by examining how trust dynamics unfold in real-world team environments. Strategies and practices that teams use to overcome barriers, leverage enablers, and cultivate the kinds of high-trust relationships essential for achieving high performance, resilience, and innovation in today's complex, interconnected work settings will be explored.

In the end, trust remains both a powerful enabler and a delicate achievement, effectively a balance between rational judgement and emotional connection, between individual agency and collective ethos. Its thoughtful cultivation is not optional but essential for organisations that aspire to create meaningful, effective, and enduring collaborations.

References

Barbalet, J. M. (1996). Social emotions: Confidence, trust and loyalty. *International Journal of Sociology and Social Policy, 16*(9/10), 75–96.

Costa, A. C. (2003). Work team trust and effectiveness. *Personnel Review, 32*(5), 605–622.

Costa, A. C., Fulmer, C. A., & Anderson, N. R. (2018). Trust in work teams: An integrative review, multilevel model, and future directions. *Journal of Organizational Behavior, 39*(2), 169–184.

Granovetter, M. S. (1973). The strength of weak ties. *American Journal of Sociology, 78*(6), 1360–1380.

Granovetter, M. (1983). The strength of weak ties: A network theory revisited. *Sociological theory*, 201–233.

Khodyakov, D. (2007). Trust as a process: A three-dimensional approach. *Sociology, 41*(1), 115–132.

Lewicki, R. J., & Bunker, B. B. (1995). *Trust in relationships: A model of development and decline.* Jossey-Bass/Wiley.

Lewicki, R. J., & Wiethoff, C. (2000). Trust, trust development, and trust repair. *The Handbook of Conflict Resolution: Theory and Practice, 1*(1), 86–107.

Mayer, R. C., Davis, J. H., & Schoorman, F. D. (1995). An integrative model of organizational trust. *Academy of Management Review, 20*(3), 709–734.

McAllister, D. J. (1995). Affect-and cognition-based trust as foundations for interpersonal cooperation in organizations. *Academy of Management Journal, 38*(1), 24–59.

McKnight, D. H. & Chervany, N. L. (1996).*The meanings of trust.* Technical report, Carlson School of Management, University of Minnesota, United States.

Mishra, A. K. (1996). Organizational responses to crisis. *Trust in Organizations: Frontiers of Theory and Research, 261*, 1996.

Rempel, J. K., Holmes, J. G., & Zanna, M. P. (1985). Trust in close relationships. *Journal of Personality and Social Psychology, 49*(1), 95.

Salas, E., Sims, D. E., & Burke, C. S. (2005). Is there a "big five" in teamwork? *Small Group Research, 36*(5), 555–599.

Shapiro, D. L., Sheppard, B. H., & Cheraskin, L. (1992). *Business on a Handshake. Negotiation Journal, 8*(4), 365–377.
Simmel, G. (1950). *The sociology of Georg Simmel* (Vol. 92892). Simon and Schuster.
Zand, D. E. (1972). Trust and managerial problem solving. *Administrative science quarterly*, 229–239.

Chapter 3
Agile and Trust: How They Intersect

Abstract Trust is the essential enabler of Agile success. It is a structural requirement for Agile teams This chapter explores how both cognitive trust (rooted in competence and reliability) and affective trust (founded on interpersonal connection and psychological safety) are operationalised in Agile frameworks, particularly Scrum. From well-defined roles and transparent artefacts to ceremonies like Retrospectives and Daily Stand-ups, Agile is intentionally designed to embed trust into everyday team practices. The chapter draws on foundational trust theories and contemporary Agile scholarship to examine how these mechanisms foster accountability, openness, and adaptability. It also considers the unique challenges of distributed teams, where trust must be cultivated through intentional practices rather than informal encounters. Ultimately, the chapter positions trust as the invisible architecture that sustains high-performing, self-organising teams. Without it, Agile degrades into superficial ritual; with it, teams can learn, innovate, and deliver with resilience and integrity.

3.1 The Nexus of Trust and Agility

Trust, as explored in the previous chapter, is a foundational element in effective collaboration, enabling individuals and teams to engage, share knowledge, and navigate uncertainty with greater ease. Both cognitive trust, grounded in rational assessments of competence and integrity, and affective trust, emerging from emotional bonds and shared experiences, are integral to fostering an environment where collaboration can thrive. Without trust, collaboration risks becoming transactional, constrained by oversight and control, and limited in its potential for creativity and adaptability.

Agile methodologies, particularly frameworks like Scrum, are designed as ecosystems that cultivate trust. Agile principles such as transparency, inspection, and adaptation are explicitly crafted to create an environment where trust is not incidental but rather operationalised through practices. Transparency, which is manifested

T. O'Connell, *Trust in Agile Teams*,
SpringerBriefs in Computer Science, https://doi.org/10.1007/978-3-032-21963-3_3

through visible backlogs, clear roles, and open communication, creates the conditions for cognitive trust by enabling rational assessments of competence and dependability. Inspection and adaptation reinforce this trust by embedding feedback loops that promote learning and accountability. Meanwhile, these same principles lay the groundwork for affective trust, as teams engage in continuous dialogue, reflect on shared experiences, and foster psychological safety.

However, while Agile principles are designed to enable trust, their success hinges on the intentionality and consistency with which they are enacted. This brings us to a critical question:

How do Agile structures and practices operationalise and sustain trust?

The following sections will examine how Agile frameworks embody trust-building mechanisms and how specific practices such as Stand-ups, Retrospectives, and Sprint Reviews foster trust over time. It is also hoped to demonstrate how organisational culture can either support or undermine these dynamics. By bridging theory and practice, it is hoped to explicate the interplay between Agile methodologies and trust as a lived experience in teams.

3.2 Trust as the Enabler of Agile Principles

Trust is a foundational enabler that operationalises Agile's core principles and values. It is not merely a byproduct of Agile ways of working. Agile methodologies, particularly Scrum, are intentionally designed to cultivate an environment where both cognitive and affective trust thrive, creating the conditions necessary for high performance, adaptability, and resilience.

3.2.1 Cognitive Trust: Underpinning Accountability and Technical Excellence

At the heart of Agile's focus on accountability and technical excellence lies cognitive trust which is the belief in a colleague's competence, reliability, and integrity. In Scrum, this trust is scaffolded through well-defined roles, with team members using transparent artefacts, and predictable processes. Roles such as Product Owner, Scrum Master, and Development Team member establish clear accountability and decision-making boundaries, reducing ambiguity and reinforcing each team member's expertise and dependability. Artefacts like the Product Backlog, Sprint Backlog, and Definition of Done make expectations explicit, track progress visibly, and offer objective benchmarks for assessing outcomes. This transparency fosters confidence that commitments will be met, and quality standards upheld. Sprint Planning and Sprint Reviews further reinforce predictability by aligning teams around shared goals and demonstrating consistent delivery, thereby enhancing cognitive trust. By reducing uncertainty and clarifying roles and expectations, these Agile structures create a dependable framework in which teams can collaborate effectively. High cognitive trust allows team members to focus on solving complex problems and delivering value, rather than expending energy managing ambiguity or second-guessing each other's capabilities.

3.2.2 *Affective Trust: Enabling Psychological Safety, Openness, and Feedback*

While cognitive trust establishes a foundation of predictability and competence, affective trust, which is rooted in interpersonal bonds, empathy, and mutual respect is essential for sustaining psychological safety and a culture of openness. Agile's emphasis on collaboration, reflection, and continuous improvement aligns with this form of trust. Scrum values such as respect, courage, openness, commitment, and focus encourage team members to engage with each other as whole individuals, acknowledging both professional skills and personal perspectives. The Agile Manifesto's core principle of "*individuals and interactions over processes and tools*" highlights the primacy of human relationships and emotional connections in effective collaboration (Beck et al., 2001). Ceremonies like Retrospectives provide a formal space for affective trust to flourish, allowing teams to surface challenges, admit vulnerabilities, and co-create solutions without fear of blame or reprisal. Daily Stand-ups and collaborative work practices promote regular interactions that build familiarity, empathy, and mutual care, all of which are critical components of affective trust. This affective dimension of trust nurtures psychological safety, where team members feel empowered to voice concerns, share incomplete ideas, and ask for help. It enables teams to adapt quickly to change, address conflicts constructively, and sustain resilience under pressure.

3.2.3 *Integrating Cognitive and Affective Trust into Agile Principles*

The dynamic interplay of cognitive and affective trust is what makes Agile truly effective. Agile principles such as transparency, inspection, and adaptation rely on cognitive trust to ensure accountability and reliability. Simultaneously, values like respect, openness, and courage depend on affective trust to foster a supportive and innovative culture. When both forms of trust are cultivated intentionally, Agile teams can navigate complexity with confidence. By engaging in honest dialogue, they can continuously improve performance. In summary, trust is far more than an emergent property of Agile practices. It is a critical enabler that brings Agile's values and principles to life. By embedding mechanisms that foster cognitive and affective trust, Agile frameworks create the psychological, social, and structural conditions for collaborative success.

3.3 Trust in Agile Team Structures

The structure of Agile teams, in particularly those that follow the Scrum framework, plays a crucial role in facilitating the development and maintenance of trust. In addition to reorganising workflow, Agile fundamentally reshapes interpersonal dynamics by decentralising authority, promoting peer interdependence, and encouraging role-based clarity. In such an environment, trust emerges as a structural and relational necessity rather than a peripheral ideal.

3.3.1 Self-Organising Teams and the Dual Nature of Trust

A defining feature of Agile software teams is their self-organising nature, where decision-making authority resides not with external managers, but with the team itself. As Highsmith (2009) observes, self-organising teams manage their own workload, reallocate tasks based on evolving needs, and jointly make decisions about execution. This shift from top-down control to team-centred governance requires team members to trust each other both cognitively and affectively.

Cognitive trust refers to confidence in a colleague's technical ability, task reliability, and domain expertise (McAllister, 1995). In the author's experience team members tend to feel that while competence is an essential baseline trait, it is the reputation for follow-through and reliability that truly establishes cognitive trust. Frequently, it is not simply competence that engenders trust, but rather the *perception* of competence over time, shaped by repeated interactions.

Conversely, affective trust stems from interpersonal bonds, shared goals, and mutual care. Team members tend to value other team members who are willing to admit vulnerability by acknowledging when they need help. Such vulnerability can be described as a catalyst for trust. When a request for help is met with support rather than judgment, trust deepens and the team's capacity for collective accountability grows Thus it may be summarised that asking for help leads to learning, which enhances competence. In effect, a virtuous cycle between affective support and cognitive trust is initiated.

In Scrum, this dynamic is reinforced structurally. Team members are bound together by the Sprint Goal and co-responsibility for delivering potentially shippable increments. The shared mental model (Levesque et al., 2001) becomes the cognitive framework around which trust can form, while shared Sprint rituals like Daily Standups and Retrospectives serve as recurring trust checkpoints.

3.4 Role Clarity and Trust through Structure

Another mechanism by which trust is facilitated in Agile teams is through explicit role definition. There are three core Scrum roles: Product Owner, Scrum Master, and Development Team. In the Scrum framework each has distinct responsibilities and accountabilities. This role clarity mitigates ambiguity and reduces conflict, both of which are known inhibitors of trust in group settings.

Contrast with traditional "manager-led teams" where direction, performance assessment, and planning are all externally controlled (Cobb, 2011). In Scrum, the Product Owner ensures that the team's effort is aligned with stakeholder needs and business value. The Scrum Master protects the process and cultivates an environment of psychological safety, while the Development Team self-organises to deliver on Sprint commitments. This separation of concerns prevents overlapping responsibilities and supports role-based trust, whereby individuals trust others to fulfil their designated function without micromanagement.

This trust is not merely procedural but has emotional and relational consequences. When team members understand not only *what* they are accountable for but also *what others* are reliably handling, the conditions for both cognitive and affective trust are strengthened.

3.5 Trust Challenges in Distributed Agile Teams

The Agile Manifesto (Beck et al., 2001) emphasises "*individuals and interactions over processes and tools,*" but this ideal is challenged in distributed Scrum teams, where face-to-face interaction is limited or absent. Geographic and temporal separation can constrain informal communication, hinder relationship development, and delay conflict resolution, all of which are vital to trust formation.

Trust in distributed teams is harder to cultivate because both indicators of reliability (e.g., meeting deadlines) and indications of care and commitment (e.g., tone, empathy) are attenuated or lost entirely in asynchronous or text-based communication. This leads to the risk that affective trust may erode in the absence of visible social signals.

Moreover, informal mentoring, a key enabler of learning and trust in co-located Scrum teams, is less likely to occur organically in remote settings. Junior developers often gain trust and competence through shadowing or collaborating with more experienced colleagues. These are interactions that are difficult to replicate virtually without intentional scaffolding.

To compensate, distributed teams can adopt deliberate trust-building strategies:

- Increase transparency through shared tools (e.g., digital boards, version control).
- Structure feedback mechanisms to replicate informal praise and guidance.
- Schedule one-on-one check-ins to foster relational trust.

Despite these efforts, it is important to acknowledge the latent fragility of trust in distributed contexts. In distributed team scenarios trust is built slower but can be lost faster online. This reinforces the need for teams to invest in proactive trust maintenance.

3.6 Agile Practices as Trust-Building Mechanisms

Agile frameworks, especially Scrum, embed practices specifically designed to cultivate and sustain trust. These mechanisms enable teams to align on goals, deliver value iteratively, and ultimately adapt to change with confidence. In Agile software development, particularly in Scrum, trust tends to operate on the two interwoven dimensions of cognitive trust and affective trust. Understanding this duality is essential to appreciating why trust is not merely a cultural lubricant but rather is a structural necessity for high-performing teams.

Cognitive trust arises from a belief in a colleague's competence, reliability, and professionalism. It forms when team members consistently deliver on commitments, possess demonstrable expertise, and exhibit predictable behaviour. Scrum reinforces cognitive trust through clear role definitions, transparent artefacts like burn-down charts, and structured events such as Sprint Planning and Reviews. These mechanisms reduce ambiguity and create a dependable framework within which individuals can operate, fostering confidence in each other's capabilities.

However, Agile teams depend on more than cognitive trust. Affective trust, rooted in interpersonal bonds and emotional connections, is equally vital. This form of trust emerges from shared experiences, empathy, mutual respect, and psychological safety. When affective trust is present, team members feel safe to admit uncertainties, voice dissenting opinions, and ask for help. These are actions that are crucial in the fast-paced, iterative cycles of Scrum. High levels of affective trust encourage open communication and a sense of belonging, both of which are indispensable for navigating the complexities of collaborative software development.

The interplay between cognitive and affective trust is particularly evident in the dynamics of self-organising teams. Cognitive trust ensures that each member is seen as competent and dependable, while affective trust creates a safe space for vulnerability and honest dialogue. Together, they enable teams to tackle complex challenges, adapt to change, and maintain high levels of performance. Without cognitive trust, coordination falters; without affective trust, collaboration breaks down.

Scrum's emphasis on transparency, role clarity, and continuous feedback supports the development of both trust types. Structured ceremonies like Daily Stand-ups foster visibility and dependability (cognitive trust), while Sprint Reviews reinforce transparency and shared achievements (both cognitive and affective trust). Retrospectives, in particular, cultivate openness, vulnerability, and shared learning which are hallmarks of affective trust. By explicitly designing opportunities for reflection and feedback, Scrum creates an environment where both task competence and emotional safety are continuously reinforced.

Additionally, the use of Definition of Done, Sprint Backlogs, and visible progress tracking e.g. Scrum Boards, Burn-Down charts, Burn-Up charts etc. further strengthens cognitive trust by making expectations explicit and outcomes verifiable. This transparency ensures that team members can rely on one another to meet shared standards, reducing ambiguity and enhancing mutual confidence.

3.7 Agile Team Structures and Trust

Agile frameworks, especially Scrum, are fundamentally structured to operationalise and sustain both cognitive and affective trust within high-performing teams. Trust is not incidental but is, instead, a designed feature of Agile systems, built into roles, artefacts, and ceremonies to create an environment conducive to collaboration, adaptability, and continuous improvement.

At the core of Agile is cognitive trust: the belief that team members possess the competence, reliability, and integrity necessary to fulfil their commitments. Agile addresses this through explicit role definitions viz. Product Owner, Scrum Master, and Development Team, all of which clarify decision-making authority and accountability. The Scrum Master facilitates team processes and removes obstacles, the Product Owner sets clear priorities and ensures alignment with business goals, and the Development Team collaboratively delivers the product increment. This clarity reflects the Agile principle of *"project success depends on motivated individuals*" and *"trust them to get the job done,"* which reduces ambiguity and fosters confidence in each member's abilities.

Agile artefacts such as the Product Backlog, Sprint Backlog, and the Definition of Done reinforce cognitive trust by making expectations transparent and progress visible. The Agile Manifesto's focus on *"working software as the primary measure of progress*" is operationalised here, i.e. visible, tangible outputs reduce uncertainty and enable rational assessments of team competence. Scrum ceremonies viz. Sprint Planning, Daily Stand-ups, Sprint Reviews all provide consistent checkpoints where commitments are reviewed, progress is validated, and adjustments are made. These structured interactions embody the principles of transparency, inspection, and adaptation, enabling teams to align expectations, clarify responsibilities, and build dependable working relationships.

However, cognitive trust alone is insufficient for Agile teams to thrive. Affective trust, which emerges from shared experiences, empathy, and mutual respect, is equally essential. Agile values of respect, openness, courage, commitment, and focus explicitly promote the interpersonal connections and psychological safety necessary for affective trust to flourish. The Agile Manifesto's principle of "*individuals and interactions over processes and tools"* highlights the primacy of human relationships in successful collaboration.

Ceremonies like Retrospectives provide formal spaces where affective trust can be built and reinforced. These sessions enable teams to surface issues and challenges, share vulnerabilities, and collaboratively develop solutions, without fear of blame or reprisal. Regular Daily Stand-ups and informal interactions further nurture affective trust by creating opportunities for connection, empathy, and shared understanding. These interactions align with Agile's emphasis on *"face-to-face conversation as the most efficient and effective method of conveying information,"* fostering psychological safety and emotional bonds that enable team resilience.

In distributed or remote Agile teams, the challenge of sustaining both cognitive and affective trust is heightened. Agile principles emphasize simplicity, directness, and transparency, qualities that may be harder to maintain across geographical and cultural divides. Tools and virtual collaboration platforms can support visibility and coordination, but they cannot fully replicate the informal interactions that build emotional connection and trust. Agile leaders must therefore be proactive in fostering personal connections, cultural competence, and clarity in distributed contexts.

Ultimately, in addition to being mechanisms for project delivery, Agile structures are scaffolds for trust. By embedding role clarity, transparency, continuous feedback, and human-centred values into the fabric of team operations, Agile frameworks create the conditions where trust can take root and flourish.

3.8 Trust Vulnerabilities in Agile Contexts

Despite Agile's explicit design to cultivate trust, several vulnerabilities can undermine it, particularly when core principles are neglected or inconsistently applied. These vulnerabilities reveal the delicate balance that Agile teams must navigate to sustain both cognitive and affective trust over time.

One significant vulnerability arises from performance pressures and delivery deadlines. While Agile emphasises adaptability and sustainable pace, teams often face competing demands that prioritise delivery over psychological safety. This can result in teams focusing too much on cognitive trust, based on competence and reliability, while neglecting the affective trust that fosters open communication and resilience. When teams feel pressure to deliver at any cost, individuals may withhold concerns, avoid difficult conversations, and default to self-protective behaviours, eroding the collaborative ethos that Agile values promote. This tension contradicts the Agile principle of *"sustainable development,"* where teams are expected to maintain a constant pace without burnout or fear.

Role ambiguity or weak leadership further exacerbate trust vulnerabilities. Agile depends on clearly defined roles and decision rights to minimise confusion and foster confidence. When roles are poorly communicated, or when Scrum Masters and Product Owners fail to uphold their responsibilities, trust falters. Team members may become uncertain about their responsibilities, leading to missed expectations, duplicated efforts, and ultimately, strained relationships. Agile principles of *transparency* and *empowerment* are compromised, resulting in a breakdown of both cognitive and affective trust.

Tacit knowledge hoarding poses another critical challenge. Agile frameworks, with their emphasis on *"continuous attention to technical excellence and good design,"* require open sharing of knowledge, particularly tacit knowledge which is embedded in individual expertise. Yet, in practice, knowledge silos often persist, driven by personal insecurities, job protection concerns, or cultural norms that discourage sharing. This behaviour undermines cognitive trust by creating dependencies on inaccessible expertise and erodes affective trust by signalling a lack of openness and collaborative spirit.

Cultural differences, especially in global or distributed teams, introduce further complexities. Agile's emphasis on simplicity, direct communication, and transparency may clash with cultural norms that prioritise hierarchy, indirectness, or deference to authority. Misunderstandings, unspoken tensions, and communication gaps can arise, undermining both clarity and psychological safety. Agile's principle of *"simplicity—the art of maximizing the amount of work not done"* may inadvertently be compromised as teams struggle to align around shared mental models in culturally diverse settings.

3.9 The Dynamic Interplay of Trust in Agile

Agile teams thrive, or fail to thrive, based on the quality of trust circulating within and between them. Trust is a dynamic, evolving phenomenon shaped by repeated interactions, shared goals, and adaptive learning. It is not a static resource. To explain this complexity, two complementary lenses can be used: the first is Lewicki and Bunker's developmental stages of trust and the second is McKnight and Chervany's model of trust constructs which examines how these constructs map onto the rhythms of Agile practices.

3.9.1 Evolving Trust: Revisiting Lewicki and Bunker in Agile Contexts

As alluded to in Chap. 2, Lewicki and Bunker (1996) identify three developmental stages of trust which are: calculus-based, knowledge-based, and identification-based. Each stage is progressively deeper in relational complexity. In Agile teams, these stages can be observed not as a linear path, but as cyclical, adaptive phases that reflect both cognitive and affective trust.

Calculus-based trust typically anchors the early stages of Agile team formation. Members assess each other's reliability based on formal roles, visible accountability structures (e.g., Sprint Reviews, task boards, etc.), and adherence to Scrum ceremonies. Cognitive trust predominates here as it is built on predictability and contract-like obligations.

As teams collaborate over successive Sprints, knowledge-based trust emerges. Team members begin to understand one another's competencies, communication styles, and problem-solving approaches. Retrospectives play a key role in this phase, enabling reflective dialogue that strengthens cognitive trust while slowly opening space for affective trust. Team members demonstrate the willingness to be vulnerable, to admit failure, and to seek help.

In high-performing Agile teams, identification-based trust arises when individuals internalise shared values and goals to the point that "*my success*" becomes "*our success.*" Affective trust takes centre stage here, enabling seamless collaboration, mutual adaptation, and collective ownership. Psychological safety becomes a lived norm rather than a stated goal.

Agile's iterative nature means that trust can regress or rebound, depending on how the team navigates conflict, change, and pressure. Trust, then, is constantly renegotiated.

3.9.2 Trust in Action: Applying McKnight and Chervany's Constructs

While Lewicki and Bunker explain how trust evolves, McKnight and Chervany (1996) offer a framework to dissect the mechanisms by which trust operates. These mechanisms are beliefs, intentions, and behaviours. When applied to Agile, these constructs illuminate how trust shapes (and is shaped by) daily practices.

Trusting beliefs in Agile relate to perceptions of others' competence, integrity, and benevolence. For instance, a developer may hold a trusting belief that the product owner will prioritise work transparently and in the team's interest. Such beliefs are often reinforced (or eroded) through rituals like Backlog Grooming or Sprint planning.

Trusting intentions involve a readiness to depend on others. When a Scrum Master delegates retrospective facilitation to a junior team member, or when a tester decides to wait for a developer's fix rather than micromanage, these illustrate intentions to rely on someone which involves a leap of faith that serves to strengthen relational bonds.

Trust-related behaviours are the most visible: open communication, constructive dissent during Daily Stand-ups, or a team's collective decision to swarm on a blocker. Agile ceremonies become stages where trust behaviours are performed, observed, and reinforced. Over time, consistent trust behaviours become cultural norms, shaping team identity.

Together, these constructs interact in feedback loops. Positive beliefs fuel trusting intentions, which foster trust-related behaviours, which then reinforce or reshape beliefs. Agile frameworks, with their emphasis on transparency, inspection, and adaptation, effectively act as trust incubators

3.10 Strategies for Cultivating Trust in Agile Teams

Trust is not merely an organic outcome of Agile work. It must be deliberately cultivated. While Agile frameworks offer structural opportunities for trust-building, these need to be animated by intentional practices and leadership behaviours. This section outlines four key strategies to deepen trust within Agile teams and closes with a comparative lens on co-located and distributed contexts.

3.10.1 Intentional Role Clarification and Onboarding

In the early stages of team formation, members may be unfamiliar with Agile and/or with each other. This ambiguity can breed mistrust. Teams benefit from clearly articulated roles, responsibilities, and mutual expectations. To assist in building trust in the early stages consider:

- Creating onboarding pathways that go beyond logistics to include Agile values, ceremonies, and norms.
- Using role clarification workshops e.g., Responsibility Assignment Matrices or Role Expectation Mapping, to distinguish accountability from contribution.
- Inviting all members, including product owners and stakeholders, to co-define *what good collaboration looks like.*

By reducing uncertainty and aligning on expectations, this strategy lays the cognitive foundation of trust and accelerates the shift from calculus-based to knowledge-based trust (Lewicki & Bunker, 1996).

3.10.2 Regular, Meaningful Retrospectives

Retrospectives can sometimes become mechanical or surface-level. To serve as trust accelerators, they must be psychologically safe spaces for real dialogue. To create the conditions for team members to feel this psychological safety, consider:

- Framing Retrospectives as opportunities to not just fix process gaps, but to listen deeply, acknowledge emotional undercurrents, and repair ruptures.
- Using facilitation techniques that invite quieter voices e.g., silent writing, anonymous input tools and encouragement of reflective inquiry.
- Embedding follow-through mechanisms: when team concerns are acted on, belief in fairness and reliability grows (McKnight and Chervany's trusting beliefs).

Meaningful retrospectives help convert emotional exposure into mutual confidence. This reinforces both affective trust and team resilience.

3.10.3 Leadership Behaviours that Model Vulnerability and Openness

Formal or informal leaders play a pivotal role in setting the emotional tone of a team. Trust flourishes when leaders model authenticity, humility, and openness to feedback. Consider:

- Admitting mistakes publicly and inviting critique e.g. *"here's what I could've done better this Sprint..."*.
- Sharing learning moments rather than only success stories.
- Demonstrating reliance on team members, reinforcing the trusting intention that "*I believe you've got this.*"

These behaviours create a climate where it is safe to experiment, dissent, and co-own outcomes which are the hallmarks of identification-based trust.

3.10.4 Support for Cross-functional Learning and Tacit Knowledge Sharing

Agile teams are inherently cross-functional, but true synergy emerges when members learn *from* each other, not just *with* each other. To facilitate this interdependent learning environment, consider:

- Implementing practices such as pair programming, cross-role shadowing, or 'Lunch and Learn' sessions that surface tacit knowledge.
- Making knowledge-sharing a Sprint deliverable: not just *what* got done, but *what was learned and transferred.*
- Rewarding curiosity and teaching, not just velocity.

This fosters competence-based beliefs while strengthening relational bonds across roles, enhancing team-wide mutual reliance and shared identity.

3.11 Trust in Co-located vs. Distributed Agile Teams: A Comparison

While the core principles of trust apply across settings, the means of cultivating trust differ based on team distribution. Consider the Table 3.1 which serves as a comparison of co-located and distributed Agile teams across four key relational aspects that influence the cultivation of trust. Each row highlights how specific conditions in different team environments affect the development and maintenance of trust:

Table 3.1 A Comparison of co-located versus distributed teams across relational aspects

Aspect	Co-located teams	Distributed teams
Spontaneity of interaction	High: trust can build through informal methods e.g. water cooler chats	Low: requires intentional structured connection
Visibility of effort	Physical cues and in-person collaboration make all contributions visible	Digital transparency is required (e.g. asynchronous updates or visible Kanban)
Social bonding	Affective trust is easier to develop through shared physical presence	Must be engineered through virtual rituals (e.g. remote coffee chats)
Conflict navigation	Nuanced, real-time feedback can help to defuse tensions when they arise	Greater potential for misinterpretation so consequently requires explicit communication norms

In distributed teams, trust must be made visible. It cannot be assumed. Practices like video-enabled Stand-ups, asynchronous appreciation threads, and shared digital whiteboards help bridge the affective and cognitive gaps.

3.12 Trust as the Lifeblood of Agile Success

Successful Agile is meant to be responsive, and team driven. Trust can be thought of as being the oil in the machine enabling coherence and resilience in every interaction. Trust is the precondition for Agile to function effectively. It is not a fortunate side effect of Agile done well.

Throughout this chapter, it has been shown that:

- Trust in Agile teams is both cognitive and affective, evolving through stages that can regress or deepen over time as explored through Lewicki and Bunker's model.
- Trust operates through a triad of mechanisms: beliefs, intentions, and behaviours, as outlined by McKnight and Chervany, all of which are made visible in Agile rituals, language, and norms.
- High-functioning Agile teams don't leave trust to chance, instead they cultivate it deliberately, through clarity, retrospection, vulnerability, and knowledge-sharing.
- rust-building is shaped by context: co-located teams may benefit from organic interactions, while distributed teams must construct intimacy and visibility more intentionally.

Ultimately, trust is the invisible architecture that supports adaptability under pressure, creativity under constraint, and collaboration amid uncertainty. It enables Agile teams to shift from compliance-driven delivery to purpose-driven performance, where individuals choose to engage deeply because they trust one another and the system of which they are a part.

Trust, in effect, is a strategic capability. Teams with high trust recover faster from setbacks, learn more efficiently, and make better decisions under time pressure. The Agile Manifesto's emphasis on individuals and interactions over processes and tools is far more than just philosophical, it is psychologically grounded in the trust that allows such interactions to be open, adaptive, and generative.

3.13 Concluding Remarks

Trust lies at the very heart of Agile's promise to foster collaboration, adaptability, and high performance. Trust is not an incidental benefit, rather it is the very foundation upon which Agile frameworks are built. This chapter has hopefully demonstrated that Agile principles and practices are explicitly designed to cultivate and sustain trust, operationalising it through clear structures, defined roles, transparent artefacts, iterative ceremonies, and cultural norms.

Trust in Agile teams is a multifaceted phenomenon encompassing both cognitive trust which is rooted in confidence in competence, reliability, and accountability, and affective trust, which emerges from emotional bonds, mutual respect, and psychological safety. Cognitive trust, reinforced by role clarity, transparent processes, and visible commitments, enables teams to navigate complexity with predictability and confidence. It forms the scaffolding upon which high-performing teams build technical excellence, accountability, and continuous delivery.

Equally vital is affective trust, the emotional glue that binds teams together. Agile creates spaces where psychological safety, empathy, and mutual care flourish, encouraging team members to express doubts, share incomplete ideas, and engage in courageous, constructive dialogue. Scrum values such as openness, respect, and courage, alongside the Agile Manifesto's emphasis on *"individuals and interactions over processes and tools,"* elevate human connection, thus allowing teams to thrive even under pressure. This dual emphasis on rational assurance and emotional connection equips Agile teams to adapt, learn, and innovate in dynamic environments.

The self-organising nature of Agile teams further amplifies the necessity of trust, as decision-making shifts from hierarchical control toward peer interdependence. While co-located teams benefit from informal interactions that organically build affective trust, distributed teams face unique challenges due to reduced social cues and fewer spontaneous exchanges. These circumstances demand intentional strategies, such as enhanced transparency, structured feedback, and proactive relational engagement, to maintain both cognitive and affective trust.

Yet, trust in Agile contexts can be vulnerable. Performance pressures, role ambiguity, knowledge silos, and cultural misalignments can erode trust, undermining the collaborative ethos central to Agile. Importantly, these vulnerabilities do not stem from Agile frameworks themselves but often arise from lapses in practice, cultural insensitivity, or misaligned priorities. Trust must therefore be deliberately nurtured through clear role delineation, continuous feedback, supportive leadership, open communication, and a commitment to cultural competence.

Ultimately, this chapter has framed trust as both a mechanism and an outcome within Agile methodologies. Agile principles of transparency, inspection, and adaptation operate effectively only when underpinned by trust, while Agile values flourish through psychological safety and authentic relationships. Trust in Agile is a dynamic, evolving interplay of cognitive and affective dimensions that enables teams to respond effectively to change, manage complexity, and sustain high performance.

In the next chapter, the focus will shift to examining the barriers that disrupt trust. While Agile frameworks are designed to foster trust, organisational structures, cultural norms, and interpersonal dynamics can compromise these ideals. Chapter 4 will explore these obstacles in depth, investigating systemic and cultural factors that inhibit trust-building and proposing strategies to overcome them. This exploration will deepen our understanding of trust's complexities in practice and underscore the necessity of intentional, sustained efforts to cultivate environments where collaboration and knowledge sharing can truly thrive.

References

Beck, K., Beedle, M., Van Bennekum, A., Cockburn, A., Cunningham, W., Fowler, M., ... & Thomas, D. (2001). Manifesto for agile software development.

Cobb, A. T. (2011). *Leading project teams: The basics of project management and team leadership.* Sage Publications.

Highsmith, J. (2009). *Agile project management: Creating innovative products.* Pearson education.

Levesque, L. L., Wilson, J. M., & Wholey, D. R. (2001). Cognitive divergence and shared mental models in software development project teams. *Journal of Organizational Behavior: the International Journal of Industrial, Occupational and Organizational Psychology and Behavior, 22*(2), 135–144.

Lewicki, R., & Bunker, B. B. (1996). *Developing and Maintaining Trust in organizations: Frontiers of theory and research,* 114.

McAllister, D. J. (1995). Affect-and cognition-based trust as foundations for interpersonal cooperation in organizations. *Academy of Management Journal, 38*(1), 24–59.

McKnight, D. H., & Chervany, N. L. (1996). The *meanings of trust.* Technical report, Carlson School of Management, University of Minnesota, United States.

Chapter 4
Barriers to Trust, Collaboration, and Knowledge Sharing

Abstract Agile promises adaptability, speed, and empowered teams. However, these benefits depend on trust. Trust is the critical enabler of effective Agile practices, particularly in Scrum, where decentralised decision-making, collaboration, and feedback loops require both cognitive trust (in competence and reliability) and affective trust (in emotional safety and shared purpose). Drawing from behavioural theory and organisational culture, the chapter examines how barriers, such as role ambiguity, legacy hierarchies, cultural misalignments, and knowledge hoarding, undermine these trust dynamics. It argues that Agile fails not because of flawed ceremonies, but because trust is absent, superficial, or unsustained. Through practical strategies and cultural insight, this chapter reframes trust as organisational infrastructure which is necessary for psychological safety, collaboration, and innovation. The chapter concludes by positioning trust as the foundation of true agility: without it, Agile degrades into superficial ritual; with it, teams unlock the adaptive potential Agile was designed to realise.

4.1 Introduction

As Agile shifts the focus from rigid hierarchies to self-organising teams, it redefines not only how work is delivered, but how people relate to one another. In this setting, trust becomes an operational necessity. Without it, core Agile practices like collaboration, transparency, and continuous improvement risk becoming hollow rituals.

In Scrum, decentralised decision-making, collective ownership, and frequent feedback loops are foundational. High-trust environments make autonomy possible, support emotional resilience, and sustain commitment to shared goals. In contrast, low-trust environments distort team roles, constrain communication, and produce what might be termed 'performative agility'. Through this lens, trust emerges not as an optional soft skill, but as the critical infrastructure beneath every successful Agile implementation.

T. O'Connell, *Trust in Agile Teams*,
SpringerBriefs in Computer Science, https://doi.org/10.1007/978-3-032-21963-3_4

4.2 Organisational and Cultural Barriers in Agile Contexts

Agile methodologies, particularly Scrum, were conceived to challenge the rigid structures and process-heavy mindsets of traditional project management by emphasising adaptability, transparency, and collaboration. At their core, Agile practices are designed to foster trust, facilitate knowledge sharing, and promote high-functioning teams capable of navigating complexity and change. However, the transition from theory to practice often exposes deep-seated organisational and cultural barriers that impede these aspirations.

These barriers are not merely minor procedural issues, rather they are rooted in entrenched mindsets, legacy hierarchies, cultural misalignments, and interpersonal dynamics. Role ambiguity, inconsistent feedback, distributed teams, and resistance to collaborative ownership are not isolated issues. They often reflect broader organisational norms and cultural expectations that prioritise control, individualism, or risk aversion over collective responsibility and adaptability. Such barriers undermine the formation of cognitive trust, i.e. confidence in a colleague's competence and reliability and affective trust, i.e. the emotional bonds that foster psychological safety and resilience.

Moreover, Agile's heavy reliance on knowledge sharing, particularly tacit knowledge that is embedded in personal experience, can falter in environments where collaboration is not genuinely valued or where knowledge is hoarded due to cultural norms or individual insecurities. Tacit knowledge is personal, experience-based, and often hard to articulate, while explicit knowledge can be easily codified and shared through documents or tools Wyatt (2001). Chau et al. (2003) opine "most of the knowledge in software engineering is tacit." Cultural differences, distributed work arrangements, and hierarchical legacies exacerbate these challenges, creating friction in team dynamics and stifling the very innovation Agile seeks to unlock.

Based on the author's experience, this chapter critically examines these organisational and cultural blocks, identifying how they manifest in practice and offering strategies to overcome them. By dissecting barriers to trust, collaboration, and knowledge sharing, it becomes clear that successful Agile adoption involves mastering ceremonies and tools but is also about transforming mindsets, behaviours, and cultural assumptions that stand in the way of true agility.

4.3 Explicit Linkage Between Barriers and Organisational Culture

Organisational culture, broadly defined as the shared norms, values, beliefs, leadership behaviours, and power dynamics that shape the social and psychological environment of an organisation, plays a critical role in either facilitating or impeding change. Unlike isolated individual behaviours or ad hoc practices, organisational culture encompasses systemic, deeply embedded patterns that influence how people interact, make decisions, and approach their work. These cultural elements operate at multiple levels, from formal policies and leadership styles to informal rituals and unwritten rules. Collectively they create an environment that can either enable or reinforce barriers.

For instance, cultural competence within an organisation extends beyond individual awareness or skill; it reflects the organisation's collective openness to diversity and inclusion as core values. When cultural competence is lacking or superficial, it often signals underlying organisational norms that marginalise certain groups or perpetuate exclusionary practices. Similarly, hierarchical legacies, which are rooted in traditional power structures and authority models, manifest as cultural barriers by shaping decision-making processes and communication flows. These entrenched power dynamics often inhibit innovation, discourage dissent, and maintain status quo practices, thereby reinforcing organisational resistance to change.

By explicitly framing such issues as organisational culture challenges, the focus shifts from blaming individuals to examining systemic factors. This perspective recognises that barriers are not merely the result of isolated actions but are perpetuated through the organisational context. This can occur through the collective attitudes, leadership behaviours, and institutionalised norms that govern everyday interactions. Addressing these cultural dimensions requires deliberate strategies aimed at reshaping organisational values and power relations, fostering inclusive leadership, and creating environments where trust and cooperation can thrive.

In summary, organisational culture can function as both a container and a catalyst for barriers within organisations. Understanding this linkage is essential for developing comprehensive interventions that target the root causes of dysfunction rather than merely addressing surface symptoms. Only by confronting and transforming these deep-seated cultural factors can organisations overcome persistent blocks and move toward greater effectiveness and adaptability.

4.4 Barriers to Building Cognitive and Affective Trust in Teams

Developing both cognitive trust (confidence in competence and reliability) and affective trust (emotional bonds and shared values) in Agile teams is a delicate, iterative process. Despite Agile methodologies like Scrum being deliberately designed to foster trust through transparency, collaboration, and shared accountability, persistent organisational and cultural barriers often undermine these efforts. This section explores these barriers, drawing from real-world Agile contexts and highlighting how they disrupt collaboration and knowledge sharing.

4.4.1 Role Ambiguity and Responsibility Diffusion

Agile frameworks emphasise clearly defined roles: Product Owner, Scrum Master, Development Team in order to provide clarity and support shared mental models. However, when roles are ill-defined or ambiguously communicated, cognitive trust suffers. Team members may lack confidence in one another's capabilities or decision-making authority, leading to duplicated efforts, missed expectations, and frustration.

In traditional work groups, individuals are accountable only for their own tasks, with no real synergy (Zayed & Kamel, 2005). In Agile, this ambiguity risks reverting teams to a pseudo-Agile structure, where superficial adherence to Scrum rituals hides a breakdown in true interdependence and collaboration. Overcoming this requires reinforcing role clarity through Scrum artifacts (Product and Sprint Backlogs) and clear agreements on responsibilities during Sprint Planning.

4.4.2 Inconsistent Feedback and Recognition

Both trust types depend on consistent, constructive feedback. Agile ceremonies like Sprint Reviews and Retrospectives are designed to surface insights and celebrate achievements, fostering both task confidence and emotional bonds. Yet, when these practices are inconsistently applied or superficial, they fail to reinforce trust. A lack of timely, actionable feedback diminishes cognitive trust leading to team members questioning whether commitments will be met. Simultaneously, insufficient recognition of contributions undermines affective trust by eroding team morale and emotional safety.

4.4.3 Challenges in Distributed and Remote Teams

Agile practices thrive on co-located, high-bandwidth communication, but increasingly, teams are distributed across geographies. Physical separation can inhibit the informal, spontaneous interactions that nurture affective trust. While tools like virtual Stand-ups and chat channels attempt to bridge gaps, asynchronous communication can limit the development of shared mental models and reduce visibility into colleagues' work, undermining cognitive trust. Knowledge sharing, especially tacit knowledge, relies heavily on face-to-face interactions (Chau et al., 2003). When these are limited, teams risk siloed knowledge and fragmented collaboration, impeding both trust-building and innovation.

4.4.4 Cultural Differences and Communication Styles

Agile's emphasis on collaboration and transparency assumes shared values and expectations, yet culturally diverse teams may have misaligned communication norms and approaches to conflict resolution. For instance, team members from high-context cultures (where messages are implicit with much being conveyed by the context) might favour indirect communication, while others expect explicit clarity (Zhang et al., 2025). Such mismatches can create misunderstandings and hidden tensions, weakening both cognitive trust (clarity of roles and expectations) and affective trust (shared understanding and empathy). Trust operates differently across contexts; thus, leaders must cultivate cultural competence, ensuring adaptive practices that honour diverse perspectives and communication styles (McKnight & Chervany, 1996).

4.4.5 Pressure of Delivery Deadlines and Performance Stress

The iterative nature of Agile, coupled with tight deadlines and evolving requirements, creates high-pressure environments. Under stress, individuals may default to self-protective behaviours, for example, withholding information, micromanaging, or avoiding risks. These behaviours undermine affective trust by signalling a lack of openness and psychological safety. Meanwhile, the focus on meeting deliverables can lead to an overemphasis on cognitive trust (competence and reliability) at the expense of affective dimensions.

Both task interdependence and outcome interdependence which are critical in Scrum teams can become strained when performance pressure disrupts cooperative norms (De Dreu, 2007). This often results in fragmented teams that struggle to maintain cohesion and resilience.

4.4.6 Tacit Knowledge Hoarding

Agile frameworks, particularly Scrum, aim to minimise knowledge silos by prioritising face-to-face communication and collective ownership. However, cultural or individual tendencies to hoard tacit knowledge pose a significant barrier. This can be either for perceived job security or due to an inability to articulate it. Sometimes, team members are completely unaware of how their tacit knowledge connects to their explicit knowledge. This can lead to knowledge bottlenecks, where critical expertise is not shared, diminishing the team's adaptive capacity and eroding both cognitive and affective trust.

4.5 Overcoming the Barriers

Addressing these challenges requires intentional, sustained efforts at both the team and organisational levels. Key strategies include:

- Clarifying roles and responsibilities using Scrum artifacts (Product and Sprint Backlogs) and transparent communication during planning.
- Embedding consistent, meaningful feedback loops through ceremonies like Sprint Reviews and Retrospectives to reinforce trust.
- Facilitating informal interactions for distributed teams, e.g. virtual watercoolers, cross-time-sone pairing, or periodic face-to-face meetings.
- Fostering cultural competence through leadership training and team discussions on values, communication preferences, and conflict resolution styles.
- Balancing performance expectations with practices that protect psychological safety, ensuring that both cognitive and affective trust can flourish under pressure.
- Promoting open knowledge sharing by modelling collaborative behaviours, celebrating contributions, and providing opportunities for mentorship and cross-training.

While trust, both cognitive and affective, is foundational to Agile's collaborative ethos, it does not operate in isolation. The same organisational and cultural forces that erode trust also disrupt the collaborative practices and knowledge-sharing behaviours upon which Agile frameworks rely. When teams struggle to establish trust, they are less likely to engage in open communication, share critical insights, or coordinate effectively, all behaviours which are essential for delivering continuous value in Agile contexts. The challenges of fragmented expertise, communication silos, and cultural misalignments inhibit trust formation but also impede the dynamic exchange of explicit and tacit knowledge that fuels innovation and adaptive problem-solving. The next section delves deeper into these interconnected barriers to collaboration and knowledge sharing, revealing how they compound trust deficits and threaten the very agility that teams strive to achieve.

4.6 Barriers to Collaboration and Knowledge Sharing

Effective collaboration and knowledge sharing are essential for high-performing Agile teams, enabling continuous delivery of value and innovative solutions. However, several systemic and cultural obstacles can impede these processes, reducing team cohesion and performance.

4.6.1 Fragmented Expertise and Knowledge Silos

One of the core challenges in Agile environments is the risk of fragmented expertise and knowledge hoarding. Tacit knowledge frequently in the guise of personal, experience-based knowledge that is difficult to articulate, often resides within individuals rather than being openly shared (Chau et al., 2003; Mahroeian & Forozia, 2012). This tacit knowledge encompasses coding conventions, system insights, and informal solutions that, when hoarded, create knowledge bottlenecks. Team members may either struggle to articulate this knowledge or deliberately withhold it for reasons such as perceived job security or mistrust.

4.6.2 Role Specialisation and Lack of Cross-Training

Scrum teams, while cross-functional, often feature members with highly specialised roles e.g. front-end developers, back-end specialists, testers, etc., each with deep expertise in their domain (Bannink, 2014). This specialisation, when not balanced with shared learning and role flexibility, fosters dependencies and limits the team's ability to collaborate effectively. The lack of cross-training means that when a key expert is unavailable, progress can stall, causing delays and frustration.

4.6.3 Communication Gaps in Distributed Teams

Distributed Agile teams face added challenges in sharing knowledge due to reduced opportunities for informal interactions. The absence of co-located, face-to-face conversations makes it difficult to surface and share tacit knowledge, which often emerges organically during informal exchanges or collaborative problem-solving (Bannerman et al., 2012). Despite the use of virtual collaboration tools, asynchronous communication can slow decision-making and create information silos.

4.6.4 Absence of Shared Mental Models

Collaboration is most effective when teams share a collective understanding of goals, roles, and processes, referred to as a shared mental model (Levesque et al., 2001). However, when teams lack this shared vision, whether due to insufficient planning, communication breakdowns, or high staff turnover, collaboration falters. Agile teams must constantly negotiate shared understandings about project goals, system requirements, individual responsibilities, and progress (Moe et al., 2010). Without this alignment, task duplication, miscommunication, and missed dependencies become common.

4.6.5 Hierarchical Mindsets and Resistance to Collective Ownership

Transitioning from traditional, hierarchical management structures to Agile's emphasis on self-organisation and shared decision-making can be challenging (Moe et al., 2010). Legacy mindsets, where managers control decisions and information flow, may persist. In such environments, team members may be reluctant to share knowledge or take ownership of collective goals, fearing blame or reprisal. This resistance undermines the collaborative ethos of Agile and perpetuates information inequalities.

4.6.6 Inadequate Collaboration Rituals

Agile frameworks encourage regular collaboration through events like Daily Stand-ups, Retrospectives, and Sprint Planning. However, when these are treated as perfunctory exercises rather than meaningful engagements, opportunities for real knowledge sharing are lost. While Agile reduces documentation requirements to encourage direct communication, this shift is only effective if supported by a collaborative culture where open discussion and idea exchange are the norm (Chau et al., 2003).

4.7 Role of Leadership and Change Management

In Agile environments, leadership extends far beyond delegating authority or decentralising control. It fundamentally shapes the culture within which Agile teams operate. Leaders are the architects of trust, collaboration, and psychological safety, setting the tone through their behaviours, attitudes, and priorities. Effective Agile leadership models an open mindset, actively encourages experimentation, and treats failure not as a fault but as a vital learning opportunity. This cultural framing fosters resilience and continuous improvement, core tenets of Agile practice.

Crucially, leaders must engage in dismantling legacy power structures that perpetuate hierarchical control, information hoarding, and resistance to shared ownership. By challenging entrenched norms and redistributing decision-making authority, leaders can create the conditions for genuine self-organisation and collective responsibility. However, this transformation demands deliberate change management strategies that recognise culture as the backbone of sustainable Agile adoption.

Ongoing coaching and leadership development are essential components of this change journey. Leaders require support and training to unlearn traditional command-and-control habits and to cultivate skills that foster inclusive communication, empathetic listening, and adaptive conflict resolution. These capabilities directly influence psychological safety, in order for team members to feel secure in voicing ideas and concerns without fear of reprisal, This, in turn, enhances knowledge sharing and cross-functional collaboration.

Moreover, aligning organisational incentives and performance metrics with Agile values reinforces these cultural shifts. When leaders prioritise collaboration, learning, and innovation in evaluation and reward systems, they signal a clear commitment to Agile principles, motivating teams to embody these behaviours consistently.

Ultimately, leadership is both the implementer and the guardian of Agile culture. The behaviours and practices leaders adopt ripple through the organisation, either enabling or obstructing trust, collaboration, and the transformative power of Agile frameworks. Without intentional, culturally attuned leadership and robust change management, Agile adoption risks being superficial i.e. limited to ceremonies and processes rather than becoming a deeply embedded organisational capability.

4.8 Psychological Safety—A Deeper Dive

Psychological safety has emerged as a key factor in effective team performance, particularly in settings such as Agile teams which depend on open communication, continuous learning, and collaborative problem-solving. At its essence, psychological safety reflects a shared belief that a team or group environment is safe for interpersonal risk-taking (Edmondson & Mogelof, 2006). Team members feel comfortable expressing ideas, admitting mistakes, asking questions, or challenging assumptions without fear of ridicule or retribution.

Understanding psychological safety is greatly enriched by placing it within the broader landscape of interpersonal trust. Trust, in general terms, involves the willingness to be vulnerable to others based on the expectation that they will respond supportively or at least without harm. It encompasses beliefs about the predictability of others' behaviour, confidence in their reliability and integrity, and a general sense that they act with good intent.

In the development of psychological safety, team members typically go through a gradual process of assessing how others behave over time. Early on, they look for consistency and predictability in actions and communication. As positive interactions accumulate, this grows into a sense of dependability, i.e. the belief that others can be counted on in moments of need or uncertainty. When this foundation is strong, deeper trust forms, characterised by a sense of mutual faith: confidence that even in ambiguous or stressful situations, colleagues will act in ways that preserve dignity and support collective goals.

Importantly, psychological safety is not just an internal feeling; it is reinforced and made visible through behaviour. Team members who feel safe tend to take interpersonal risks by offering dissenting opinions, acknowledging limitations, or experimenting with new ideas. These behaviours, in turn, reinforce the safety of the environment, creating a positive feedback loop. Over time, the team develops a norm of openness and mutual respect.

The formation of this kind of trust-based climate depends on more than just individual disposition or personality traits. It is shaped by repeated interactions, the clarity of group norms, and the emotional tone of relationships. Particularly in high-pressure or ambiguous situations, where stakes are high and outcomes uncertain, the presence or absence of psychological safety becomes most apparent. When it is strong, teams remain cohesive and adaptive. When it is lacking, members may withdraw, self-censor, or avoid taking responsibility.

In agile settings, where collaboration is frequent and iterative work demands fast feedback and high interdependence, psychological safety underpins team effectiveness. It enables individuals to contribute fully, challenge the status quo, and learn from failure without damaging relationships or performance. Though intangible, psychological safety acts as a kind of social infrastructure. Once present, it allows trust to flourish and innovation to emerge.

Psychological safety can be measured through anonymous team surveys, pulse checks, or structured Retrospectives that invite honest reflection on team dynamics. Tools like Google's re: Work framework or Edmondson's Team Survey can help teams assess and improve their climate for safety and trust.

4.9 Navigating and Overcoming the Barriers

Overcoming the multifaceted barriers to trust, collaboration, and knowledge sharing in Agile environments requires deliberate and sustained effort. Success hinges on intentionally designing collaborative practices that go beyond formal processes to foster genuine connection, clarity, and cultural alignment within teams and across organisations. Strategies to be considered include:

4.9.1 Clarifying Roles and Responsibilities

Barriers can be overcome by establishing clear, well-communicated roles and responsibilities. Leveraging Scrum artifacts such as Product and Sprint Backlogs, alongside transparent planning sessions, helps establish shared expectations and reduces ambiguity. This clarity builds cognitive trust by ensuring that team members understand each other's accountabilities and decision-making authority, preventing overlap and frustration.

4.9.2 Embedding Consistent and Meaningful Feedback

Agile ceremonies, such as Sprint Reviews, Retrospectives, and Daily Stand-ups, must transcend rote ritual to become purposeful forums for timely, constructive feedback and recognition. Consistent feedback reinforces both cognitive and affective trust by affirming competence and nurturing psychological safety, enabling teams to adapt and grow.

4.9.3 Facilitating Informal and Structured Interactions in Distributed Teams

Physical separation in distributed or hybrid teams creates challenges for spontaneous knowledge sharing and trust-building. Intentional facilitation of informal interactions, such as virtual coffee breaks or peer discussion sessions, recreates the rich social context necessary for surfacing tacit knowledge. Alongside this, structured practices like cross-time-zone pairing and regular check-ins maintain alignment and cohesion.

4.9.4 Encouraging Cross-Functional Learning and Knowledge Sharing

Promoting cross-functional learning through pair programming, mentorship programs, and dedicated knowledge-sharing sessions helps break down silos and mitigates the risks of expertise fragmentation. This not only improves team resilience and adaptability but also fosters affective trust by strengthening interpersonal bonds and shared ownership.

4.9.5 Establishing Shared Mental Models Through Continuous Dialogue

High-performing Agile teams maintain shared mental models, with common understandings of goals, roles, processes, and progress. Establishing these models requires ongoing, clear communication, supported by documented goals and continuous dialogue, ensuring alignment and preventing miscommunication.

4.9.6 Cultivating Cultural Competence and Inclusive Communication

Cultural diversity can enrich Agile teams, but only if differences in communication styles and conflict resolution are recognised and respected. Leadership must actively promote cultural competence by encouraging adaptive communication norms and fostering an inclusive environment where diverse perspectives are understood and valued. This is essential for sustaining both cognitive clarity and emotional safety.

4.9.7 Balancing Delivery Pressures with Psychological Safety

Agile's iterative, fast-paced nature can amplify stress, potentially triggering protective behaviours that erode trust. Organisations must intentionally balance performance demands with practices that safeguard psychological safety, creating environments where risk-taking, vulnerability, and open dialogue are encouraged rather than penalised.

4.9.8 Challenging Hierarchical Legacies to Empower Collective Ownership

Legacy hierarchical mindsets often resist the self-organising and collaborative ethos Agile requires. Breaking down these barriers involves empowering teams to make decisions and share ownership of outcomes, fostering autonomy while reinforcing accountability. Leaders play a critical role by modelling openness and decentralising control.

4.9.9 Reinforcing Collaboration Through Purposeful Agile Rituals

Embedding collaboration deeply into Agile rituals is crucial. Events such as Daily Stand-ups, Sprint Planning, Reviews, and Retrospectives should be carefully designed to be meaningful and inclusive, providing genuine opportunities for reflection, learning, and connection. When these ceremonies are conducted with intention, they become powerful mechanisms to sustain trust, reinforce shared goals, and cultivate a collaborative culture.

4.10 Overcoming Cultural and Systemic Barriers to Agile Success

The challenges outlined in this chapter reveal that the barriers to trust, collaboration, and knowledge sharing in Agile environments are not isolated missteps but rather, manifestations of deep-rooted cultural norms and systemic practices. Agile's promise to foster adaptability, innovation, and collective ownership, can only be fully realised when organisations confront these underlying impediments.

Cultural diversity, with its myriad communication styles, values, and conflict resolution norms, offers both richness and complexity. While diversity has the potential to fuel creativity and resilience, unmanaged cultural differences can create misunderstanding, hinder knowledge flow, and erode psychological safety. Leaders must cultivate cultural competence, promoting inclusive communication norms that honour diverse perspectives while aligning with Agile principles of transparency and collaboration. This requires intentional efforts to build shared mental models and mutual understanding, particularly in distributed or global teams where implicit cultural cues may otherwise remain unspoken.

Similarly, legacy hierarchies and entrenched mindsets can inhibit the self-organising, collaborative dynamics that Agile frameworks demand. When decision-making authority remains concentrated or when knowledge is hoarded (whether out of fear, habit, or perceived job security) teams struggle to build the cognitive and affective trust essential for high performance. Overcoming these systemic barriers often involves organisational cultural transformation. Leaders must model openness, empower cross-functional collaboration, and establish psychological safety as a foundational norm, not a peripheral ideal.

Agile practices cannot be sustained on ritual alone. Ceremonies like Daily Stand-ups, Sprint Reviews, and Retrospectives must move beyond mere formalities to become genuine forums for reflection, learning, and connection. In distributed or hybrid teams, intentional efforts to recreate the richness of informal interactions can be facilitated through virtual watercoolers, peer discussions, and face-to-face gatherings are vital to maintaining trust and knowledge flow.

4.11 Concluding Remarks

Throughout this chapter, one message has emerged consistently: trust is not a peripheral virtue in Agile. It is the strategic core around which all effective Agile practices revolve. From the early origins of Agile as a response to command-and-control rigidity, to the lived reality of Scrum ceremonies and team autonomy, trust is the essential condition that enables Agile to be more than a process. Trust creates a culture of Agility.

Cognitive trust ensures reliability and predictability, affective trust sustains psychological safety and empathy. Together, they underpin the open communication, decentralised leadership, and continuous learning that define high-performing Agile teams. Without trust, autonomy is fragile, courage is suppressed, and commitment is hollow. Teams may still "do Agile," but the spirit of Agile i.e.., the agility, adaptability, and shared ownership, is lost.

The strategic implications are clear. Agile transformation efforts must move beyond tooling and training to address the deeper behavioural and cultural dynamics at play. Organisations must deliberately cultivate trust by clarifying roles, nurturing psychological safety, rewarding collaborative behaviour, and fostering environments where risk-taking and vulnerability are not just tolerated but expected.

Trust cannot be retrofitted once dysfunction sets in. It must be foundational. Trust and collaboration practices must adapt as teams mature. Early-stage teams may need more structured rituals and explicit role definitions, while mature teams benefit from evolving norms and increased autonomy. Recognising these stages helps leaders support teams appropriately. Where trust is strong, Agile thrives. Where it is absent, Agile withers, reduced to ceremony without substance. Investing in trust is a hard strategic imperative for sustainable Agile success. It is not a soft ambition.

References

Bannerman, P. L., Hossain, E., & Jeffery, R. (2012, January). Scrum practice mitigation of global software development coordination challenges: A distinctive advantage?. In *2012 45th Hawaii International Conference on System Sciences* (pp. 5309–5318). IEEE.

Bannink, S. (2014, January). Challenges in the transition from waterfall to scrum–a case study at portbase. In *20th twente student conference on information technology* (Vol. 182).

Chau, T., Maurer, F., & Melnik, G. (2003, June). Knowledge sharing: Agile methods vs. tayloristic methods. In *WET ICE 2003. Proceedings. Twelfth IEEE International Workshops on Enabling Technologies: Infrastructure for Collaborative Enterprises, 2003.* (pp. 302–307). IEEE.

De Dreu, C. K. (2007). Cooperative outcome interdependence, task reflexivity, and team effectiveness: A motivated information processing perspective. *Journal of Applied Psychology, 92*(3), 628.

Edmondson, A. C., & Mogelof, J. P. (2006). Explaining psychological safety in innovation teams: organizational culture, team dynamics, or personality? In *Creativity and innovation in organizational teams* (pp. 129–156). Psychology Press.

Levesque, L. L., Wilson, J. M., & Wholey, D. R. (2001). Cognitive divergence and shared mental models in software development project teams. *Journal of Organizational Behavior: The International Journal of Industrial, Occupational and Organizational Psychology and Behavior, 22*(2), 135–144.

Mahroeian, H., & Forozia, A. (2012). Challenges in managing tacit knowledge: A study on difficulties in diffusion of tacit knowledge in organizations. *International Journal of Business and Social Science, 3*(19).

McKnight, D. H., & Chervany, N. L. (1996). *The meanings of trust*. Technical report, Carlson School of Management, University of Minnesota, United States.

Moe, N. B., Dingsøyr, T., & Dybå, T. (2010). A teamwork model for understanding an agile team: A case study of a Scrum project. *Information and Software Technology, 52*(5), 480–491.

Wyatt, J. C. (2001). 10. Management of explicit and tacit knowledge. *Journal of the Royal Society of Medicine*, *94*(1), 6–9.

Zayed, A. M., & Kamel, M. M. (2005). *Teams and work groups*. Cario University.

Zhang, S., de Jong, M. D., & Gosselt, J. F. (2025). Cultural differences in microblogging: How Western IT Companies adapt Twitter (X) activities to the Chinese Weibo context. *Journal of International Consumer Marketing, 37*(1), 72–87.

Chapter 5
The Power of Open Communication in Scrum Teams

Abstract Scrum is often praised for its structure and efficiency, but its true effectiveness hinges on something far less tangible: trust. This chapter explores how open communication serves as the foundation for trust in Agile teams, enabling psychological safety, team cohesion, and continuous learning. Drawing from organisational theory, behavioural science, and Agile practice, the chapter examines how trust is built through structured events and artefacts but also through day-to-day interactions marked by honesty, integrity, and transparency. It highlights the critical role of organisational culture, identifying barriers such as fear, hierarchy, and cultural silence that constrain open dialogue. Conversely, it outlines enabling conditions, like psychological safety, feedback culture, and inclusive norms, that foster trust and high performance. By distinguishing between transactional communication and transformational dialogue, and between high-trust and low-trust patterns, the chapter offers a practical lens for diagnosing team health and enhancing collaboration. Ultimately, it argues that open communication is the operating system of Agile. Without it, Scrum devolves into ritual; with it, teams unlock agility, resilience, and genuine innovation.

5.1 Introduction

In today's software development landscape, Agile methodologies have become the dominant paradigm for managing complexity, enhancing responsiveness, and accelerating value delivery. Among these methodologies, Scrum is one of the most widely adopted frameworks, offering a structured yet flexible approach centred around iterative progress, cross-functional collaboration, and continuous improvement. However, the success of Scrum does not rest solely on the implementation of its roles, events, and artifacts. Rather, it hinges on a deeper, less tangible factor: organisational culture.

Organisational culture shapes how teams think, interact, and solve problems. It comprises a set of shared assumptions that guide members of an organisation in interpreting and responding to their environment. These are assumptions that, once validated through experience, become embedded as the accepted norms of behaviour (Schein, 2010). In Agile contexts, these norms must support values such as openness,

T. O'Connell, *Trust in Agile Teams*,
SpringerBriefs in Computer Science, https://doi.org/10.1007/978-3-032-21963-3_5

adaptability, and collective responsibility. Without a cultural foundation that aligns with these principles, even the most technically proficient Scrum implementation is unlikely to thrive.

Scrum teams are particularly dependent on a supportive cultural context that encourages psychological safety and interpersonal trust. While sound processes and technical expertise are vital, it is the team's communication dynamics that often determine whether goals are achieved. Trust, in this setting, is an evolving outcome of repeated, positive interpersonal interactions characterised by honesty, transparency, and reliability. It should not be taken for granted as a fixed attribute.

Open communication is thus central to enabling trust in Scrum teams. Effective teams communicate frequently and purposefully, using both formal and informal channels to maintain alignment, share knowledge, and surface issues early. This kind of communication allows teams to adapt in real time, reduce ambiguity, and make collective decisions with confidence. When individuals feel safe to voice concerns, admit mistakes, ask for assistance, or challenge assumptions, they contribute to a climate of psychological safety. In contrast, when communication is constrained, either by fear, hierarchy, or ambiguity, trust erodes, and the team's capacity to collaborate meaningfully is diminished.

Communication in Scrum extends beyond simple information exchange. It includes active listening, clear articulation of ideas, timely feedback, and a shared commitment to transparency. Scrum artifacts, such as the Product Backlog, Sprint Backlog, and Increment, serve to make work visible and reduce uncertainty. Yet the true impact of these tools depends on how transparently they are used and whether team members are willing to engage with one another openly and constructively.

Feedback loops further reinforce this communicative culture. Events like the Sprint Review and Retrospective institutionalise reflection and adjustment, while ongoing peer-to-peer exchanges allow for real-time learning and course correction. These feedback mechanisms are essential for developing a team's capacity to self-organise and continually improve. When paired with a no-blame ethos and a shared sense of responsibility, they create fertile ground for trust to grow and sustain itself over time.

This chapter explores how open communication, which encompasses transparency, honesty, feedback, and psychological safety, enables trust in Scrum teams. Drawing on the core values of Agile and the communication structures embedded within Scrum, the chapter examines how trust is actively constructed through daily interactions. It will examine the enabling conditions for openness and the specific behaviours that make trust possible within high-functioning teams.

In a development environment characterised by constant change, distributed work, and increasing interdependence, open communication is essential. Teams that foster it are better equipped to manage complexity, integrate diverse perspectives, and deliver high-quality outcomes consistently. By understanding the mechanisms through which communication cultivates trust, organisations can more effectively support their Agile teams and unlock the full potential of the Scrum framework.

5.2 Agile Organisational Culture and Trust

Agile methodologies, and Scrum in particular, are so much more than collections of technical practices or process prescriptions; they are embedded within a broader organisational philosophy that demands a distinct cultural orientation. This cultural orientation is marked by values such as adaptability, collaboration, transparency, and continuous learning. For Scrum to operate as intended, these values must be deeply embedded in the ways individuals think, behave, and interact within their teams and organisations.

Organisational culture is often described as the 'invisible hand' guiding behaviour. It is comprised of the underlying assumptions, values, and beliefs that shape how work is approached, how success is defined, and how interpersonal dynamics unfold. When these cultural elements are aligned with Agile principles, they create an environment where teams can self-organise, respond rapidly to change, and deliver value incrementally. When they are misaligned. i.e. where hierarchy, blame, control, or opacity dominate, Agile practices are reduced to superficial rituals that fail to deliver their intended benefits.

Scrum, as a framework, depends upon a high degree of interpersonal trust and team autonomy. Unlike traditional models of software development where roles and responsibilities are clearly demarcated and tightly controlled, Scrum is based on shared ownership, collective accountability, and emergent decision-making. These features require team members to engage with one another openly, honestly, and frequently. For successful teamwork in Scrum trust is a structural necessity.

This makes the role of culture especially significant. In organisations where psychological safety is prioritised, mistakes are treated as learning opportunities, and status differences are minimised, trust is more likely to develop organically. Team members are encouraged to speak candidly, seek feedback, challenge assumptions, and take interpersonal risks, all of which contribute to a richer and more resilient collaborative environment. Conversely, in cultures where individuals are penalised for vulnerability or dissent, communication becomes guarded, innovation is stifled, and trust is undermined.

An Agile-compatible culture also facilitates transparency. This is not limited to visibility of work through artifacts like backlogs or task boards, but extends to openness in communication, clarity of expectations, and willingness to surface, what can sometimes be, uncomfortable truths. Transparency reduces ambiguity and enhances predictability, both of which are critical for fostering cognitive-based trust i.e. the belief that others are competent, reliable, and acting in good faith.

It is important to recognise that Agile culture cannot be mandated through policy or imposed through process. It is cultivated over time through consistent reinforcement of values, behaviours, and leadership practices that support openness and mutual respect. Leaders in Agile organisations must model the behaviours they wish to see. This includes engaging in honest dialogue, accepting constructive criticism, acknowledging uncertainty, and demonstrating humility. These behaviours signal to team members that communication is safe, valued, and essential for success.

Ultimately, organisational culture serves as the foundation upon which trust in Scrum teams is built. Without cultural reinforcement, the core mechanics of Scrum, i.e. the Daily Scrum, Sprint Planning, and Retrospective, risk becoming superficial exercises devoid of meaningful impact. When culture and process align, however, Scrum becomes far more than a methodology; it becomes a vehicle for building high-performing teams characterised by deep trust, shared purpose, and continuous learning.

5.3 No Blame, High Trust: Creating the Conditions for Openness

One of the most significant cultural conditions required for open communication in Scrum teams is the absence of blame. In high-trust environments, individuals feel psychologically safe to speak candidly, acknowledge mistakes, and offer dissenting views without fear of retribution or reputational damage. This sense of safety is a critical prerequisite for transparency, collaboration, and continuous learning, which are the hallmarks of effective Agile practice.

The traditional organisational response to failure often involves assigning blame and seeking individual accountability. While this may provide short-term explanations or a superficial sense of control, it undermines long-term team cohesion and stifles innovation. In contrast, Agile environments are oriented toward learning and adaptation. Failures are treated not as personal deficiencies but as opportunities to gain insight and refine both processes and assumptions. This learning-focused stance shifts the emphasis from "*who is at fault*" to "*what can we learn,*" fostering a climate in which communication remains open, even under pressure.

A no-blame culture does not imply the absence of accountability; rather, it reframes accountability as collective and forward-looking rather than punitive and retrospective. In Scrum teams, the emphasis is on shared ownership of outcomes. When an impediment or failure arises, the response is collaborative: *What went wrong? What could be improved? How can we support each other in preventing a recurrence?* This kind of inquiry invites contributions from all team members and encourages mutual responsibility rather than defensiveness or avoidance.

Establishing a no-blame culture requires active support from leadership and a deliberate focus on psychological safety. Leaders must model vulnerability, demonstrate openness to feedback, and explicitly reward honesty and constructive risk-taking. When individuals see that raising concerns or admitting uncertainty is not only permitted but encouraged, they are more likely to engage authentically and proactively in team interactions.

Importantly, the no-blame principle extends beyond formal meetings or retrospectives. It must permeate everyday interactions, becoming an ingrained aspect of team dynamics. Informal feedback, spontaneous conversations, and real-time problem solving are all more effective in an atmosphere where individuals feel free to speak without fear of negative consequences. The cumulative effect of these micro-interactions is a culture in which open communication is both a norm and an expectation.

Moreover, the no-blame ethos reinforces trust over time. Trust in Agile teams is built through consistent and credible behaviour: doing what one says, owning outcomes, and engaging transparently. When individuals experience that their honesty is met with support rather than judgement, they become more willing to trust others and contribute openly to the team's collective efforts. In this sense, psychological safety and trust are mutually reinforcing. Each deepens the other.

Creating the conditions for openness requires a fundamental shift in mindset from individual protectionism to collective learning. When teams embrace a no-blame culture, they unlock the potential for deeper collaboration, faster adaptation, and more innovative solutions. This cultural foundation is essential for sustaining the high levels of trust and open communication upon which successful Scrum implementation depends.

5.4 Transparency Through Communication

Transparency is a foundational value in Agile practice and a critical enabler of trust within Scrum teams. It refers to the clear, open, and timely sharing of information, expectations, and intentions among team members and stakeholders. In the context of Scrum, transparency is not simply about making work visible, rather it is about fostering an environment in which communication is honest, accessible, and responsive to the needs of the team.

At its core, transparency reduces uncertainty. It allows team members to understand the current state of work, identify emerging risks, and coordinate actions effectively. This clarity supports decision-making and ensures that all members of the team are working from a shared understanding. When team members have confidence that they are being kept informed, and that their input is welcomed, they are more likely to engage, contribute, and take the initiative.

Scrum provides several formal mechanisms that promote transparency. Artifacts such as the Product Backlog, Sprint Backlog, and Increment serve as shared reference points that capture scope, progress, and priorities. Events such as the Daily Scrum, Sprint Review, and Retrospective are structured opportunities to communicate status, surface impediments, and reflect on team performance. These rituals institutionalise transparency and help to normalise open dialogue as part of the team's working rhythm.

However, transparency is behavioural not procedural. Merely following Scrum's mechanical structures does not guarantee meaningful communication. Teams must also develop interpersonal habits that support transparency, such as openly discussing challenges, raising concerns early, and providing candid updates on progress. It is through these behaviours that trust is formed and reinforced. When individuals observe that others are willing to be truthful, even when the truth is uncomfortable or inconvenient, they are more likely to reciprocate, and trust grows as a result.

An important aspect of transparency is the willingness to admit when something is unclear, delayed, or going wrong. This requires vulnerability, particularly in team environments where individuals may feel pressure to demonstrate competence or meet high expectations. A culture that encourages transparency must therefore also prioritise psychological safety i.e. ensuring that openness is met with support, not blame. When it is safe to speak up, the quality of communication improves, and the team becomes more agile in identifying and addressing problems.

Transparency also extends beyond the boundaries of the Scrum team. Product Owners must communicate clearly with stakeholders about priorities, risks, and timelines. Scrum Masters must be transparent about impediments and team health. Developers must be forthcoming with each other about progress and potential issues. In this way, transparency becomes a collective practice and is embedded in every interaction and every layer of the Agile organisation.

Moreover, transparency plays a central role in building what is often referred to as cognitive trust i.e. the trust in another's competence and reliability. When information is shared openly, and team members consistently deliver what they promise or explain clearly when they cannot, they demonstrate reliability and credibility. This kind of trust forms the basis for effective delegation, reduced supervision, and stronger collaboration.

Ultimately, transparency through communication is what transforms a group of individuals into a cohesive, high-performing team. It enables teams to act with clarity, adapt with confidence, and make decisions in alignment with shared goals. As a foundational principle of both Agile and Scrum, transparency is a critical condition for trust, learning, and success in complex software development environments.

5.5 Transactional to Transformational Dialogue

While transparency is a critical foundation for trust in Scrum teams, it is important to go further and examine *how* teams communicate. Not all communication is equal in its impact. A key distinction lies between transactional communication and transformational dialogue.

Transactional communication focuses on the exchange of information i.e. status updates, task assignments, or reporting progress. It is necessary for coordination and basic visibility but tends to be one-way or minimal in depth. When Scrum events become purely transactional, they risk devolving into ritualistic check-ins that fail to surface underlying issues or challenge flawed assumptions. This can lead to misalignment, hidden risks, and a false sense of progress.

Transformational dialogue, by contrast, is inherently collaborative and generative. It is a two-way (often multi-way) process in which team members actively engage to make sense of complex problems together. It includes asking probing questions, exploring alternative perspectives, sharing uncertainties, and negotiating meaning.

This kind of communication fosters shared understanding, deeper alignment, and collective ownership of outcomes.

Transformational dialogue is what turns a collection of individual experts into a true team. It supports adaptive problem-solving by making it safe to challenge ideas, learn from mistakes, and evolve plans in real time. It also enables faster feedback cycles and better decision-making because everyone understands not just *what* is happening but *why* decisions are being made.

In Scrum, opportunities for transformational dialogue are embedded in events such as Sprint Planning (where scope, priorities, and strategies are negotiated), Sprint Reviews (where stakeholder feedback informs product evolution), and especially Retrospectives (which invite critical reflection and continuous improvement). Even the Daily Scrum, often treated as a quick status meeting, can benefit from a shift toward meaningful dialogue by surfacing blockers early and encouraging team members to support each other in real time.

In the end, whilst Scrum's promise of agility depends on transparent communication, it really depends on cultivating *transformational* conversations that help teams navigate complexity, align deeply around shared goals, and continuously learn and adapt together. Moving from mere information sharing to open, honest, and reflective dialogue is essential for building the trust and psychological safety that high-performing Agile teams require.

5.6 Feedback Loops: The Engine of Continuous Improvement

A central tenet of Agile and Scrum is the belief that learning should be continuous and that processes, products, and behaviours can always be improved through timely reflection and adaptation. Feedback loops are the structural mechanisms through which this learning occurs and from which trust is enhanced (O'Connell & Molloy, 2018). They allow teams to examine the gap between intention and outcome, make adjustments, and improve both performance and collaboration over time.

In Scrum, feedback loops are deliberately embedded into the framework through recurring events: the Daily Scrum, the Sprint Review, and the Sprint Retrospective (McHugh et al., 2011). Each of these creates a space for the team to communicate openly about progress, impediments, quality, and team functioning. These regular, time-boxed interactions ensure that feedback is not sporadic or reactive but instead proactive and rhythmic. When used effectively, they facilitate a culture of transparency, self-correction, and mutual accountability.

The Daily Scrum provides a short, focused opportunity for the team to synchronise, identify potential blockers to progress, and adapt the plan for the day. It promotes real-time situational awareness and invites team members to offer support or share critical information. The Sprint Review invites feedback from stakeholders, helping the team understand whether they are building the right product and how the product might evolve to meet changing needs. Finally, the Sprint Retrospective offers a vital opportunity for introspection. This is where the team reflects not on the work delivered, but on how they worked together. It is a space for discussing what went well, what could be improved, and what changes should be implemented in the next iteration.

Beyond these formal events, feedback should also flow continuously and informally throughout the Sprint. Ad hoc conversations, peer code reviews, one-on-one discussions, and spontaneous problem-solving interactions all serve as micro-feedback loops that enhance responsiveness and reinforce collaboration. When feedback becomes part of the team's everyday habits, as opposed to something reserved for end-of-cycle events, it contributes to a more agile, adaptable team culture.

The effectiveness of feedback loops does not just rely on frequency or structure. It depends on how feedback is given and received. For feedback to build trust, it must be timely, specific, constructive, and respectful. General or delayed feedback loses relevance and may even cause defensiveness. In contrast, feedback that is anchored in observable behaviours or outcomes, delivered with the intent to support rather than criticise, can strengthen relationships and improve performance.

Equally important is the team's receptiveness to feedback. An environment in which individuals feel safe to offer and receive feedback without fear of blame or retribution fosters trust and continuous learning. Teams that embrace feedback as a shared responsibility i.e. where giving feedback is viewed as a sign of care and accountability rather than judgment, are more likely to experience sustained improvement and stronger interpersonal bonds.

In addition, feedback loops serve an important trust-building function at the organisational level. They close the communication gap between teams and stakeholders, between intentions and impact. When feedback from customers or users is regularly incorporated into the product, it signals responsiveness and reinforces the team's sense of purpose. When leadership listens to feedback from Scrum teams and acts upon it, it builds trust vertically across the organisation.

In essence, feedback loops operationalise the Agile principle of inspect and adapt. They transform openness from a theoretical value into a practical routine. More than that, they are trust accelerators: they allow team members to demonstrate dependability, address misunderstandings before they escalate, and align expectations through dialogue rather than assumption. Over time, these interactions accumulate into a culture of trust, where open communication is the norm and continuous improvement is embedded in the team's identity.

5.7 Enabling Factors: Honesty, Integrity, and Psychological Safety

While structural elements like events and artifacts enable open communication in Scrum, it is ultimately the interpersonal dynamics and behavioural norms within the team that determine whether that communication leads to trust. Among the most critical enabling factors are honesty, integrity, and psychological safety. These qualities form the human foundation upon which trust is built and sustained over time.

Honesty is the baseline requirement for authentic communication. In Scrum teams, honesty means more than avoiding deception; it involves the full and transparent sharing of relevant information, including uncertainty, setbacks, or limitations. When team members communicate honestly, i.e. whether reporting progress, admitting a mistake, or raising a concern, they reduce ambiguity and establish a credible foundation for collaboration. In this context, honesty is not a private moral choice but a shared professional obligation. Without it, trust cannot take hold.

However, honesty must be exercised constructively. Brutal candour without empathy can alienate team members and harm psychological safety. Effective Scrum teams balance honesty with respect, using clear but considerate language to ensure that the message supports both the individual and the group. Constructive honesty builds mutual understanding, strengthens accountability, and allows the team to address issues before they escalate.

Integrity extends beyond communication into action. It is demonstrated when team members act consistently with shared values, honour their commitments, and align their behaviours with their words. In a Scrum context, integrity means doing the right thing even when it is difficult, for example, resisting shortcuts that compromise quality, acknowledging incomplete work, or pushing back on unrealistic expectations. Empirical research confirms that integrity is crucial to successful teamwork (O'Connell, 2019). When individuals demonstrate integrity, they become more predictable and dependable in the eyes of others. Predictability and dependability are two of the essential components of trust.

Integrity also plays a key role in technical and product-related decisions. Developers who take ownership of code quality, Product Owners who advocate transparently for stakeholder needs, and Scrum Masters who uphold the values of the framework all contribute to a climate of principled behaviour. Over time, this consistency fosters deep interpersonal trust and reinforces a shared team identity grounded in professional standards.

Complementing honesty and integrity is the broader condition of psychological safety, which is the belief that one can express themselves without fear of humiliation, dismissal, or retribution. Psychological safety enables the kinds of interpersonal risk-taking required for innovation and continuous improvement. It allows team members to ask questions, voice concerns, propose new ideas, and challenge assumptions, even in high-pressure situations or hierarchical settings.

A psychologically safe environment is characterised by inclusive participation, active listening, and a tolerance for imperfection. Leaders, whether formal or informal, play a pivotal role in modelling these behaviours. When they invite input, acknowledge their own limitations, and respond to feedback with openness, they signal that the team environment is one of support, not scrutiny. This, in turn, encourages others to engage more freely and contribute more fully.

Together, honesty, integrity, and psychological safety act as reinforcing mechanisms. Honesty enables clarity, integrity provides consistency, and psychological safety sustains openness. When these qualities are present, Scrum teams are more resilient, adaptive, and cohesive. Communication becomes richer and more solution-focused, and the team becomes a high-trust system capable of navigating complexity and uncertainty.

Ultimately, it is these human factors that determine whether the structural features of Scrum can achieve their intended purpose. Without them, ceremonies become performative, feedback becomes superficial, and collaboration becomes transactional. With them, however, Scrum teams are positioned to embody the full spirit of Agile, i.e. working transparently, learning continuously, and delivering value collaboratively in every iteration.

5.8 The Role of Scrum Events in Structuring Communication

While open communication in Agile teams is largely cultural and behavioural, the Scrum framework provides structured mechanisms that embed communication into the daily pattern of work. These mechanisms take the form of recurring events, each with a specific purpose, duration, and set of participants. Far from being mere administrative checkpoints, Scrum events serve as the scaffolding for transparency, alignment, and collective decision-making. When approached with intent and psychological safety, these events become vital forums for building trust and reinforcing open communication practices.

Sprint Planning is the first communication-focused event in each Scrum iteration. Its purpose is to establish a shared understanding of the work to be delivered during the Sprint and to determine how that work will be accomplished. This event facilitates collaboration between the Product Owner, who articulates the '*what*' and '*why*,' and the Development Team, who define the '*how*' and the '*how much*.' For this event to be effective, communication must be honest, expectations must be realistic, and constraints or uncertainties must be openly acknowledged. When this occurs, teams can enter the Sprint with clarity and confidence, knowing that they are aligned around a common goal.

The Daily Scrum (or Stand-Up) is perhaps the most visible example of structured communication in Scrum. Held at the same time and place each working day, this 15-min meeting allows the team to synchronise, assess progress toward the Sprint Goal, and adjust plans in response to new information. The key value of this event lies in its brevity and focus. It creates a reliable cadence of communication that prevents small issues from becoming major impediments. Moreover, the Daily Scrum fosters accountability, as each team member publicly shares what they are working on, what they have accomplished, and whether they face any obstacles. Over time, this habitual transparency builds trust and strengthens cohesion.

The Sprint Review extends communication beyond the team to include stakeholders. Its goal is to inspect the Increment, gather feedback, and determine next steps based on what was delivered. Effective Sprint Reviews are interactive dialogues. They allow stakeholders to provide meaningful input and enable the team to adjust the Product Backlog in response to real-world feedback. This visibility reinforces transparency and responsiveness, signalling to stakeholders that the team is not only delivering, but listening. Internally, the Review demonstrates that the team's work is open to scrutiny and refinement, both of which are critical markers of trustworthiness.

The Sprint Retrospective is the primary vehicle for reflective communication. It provides the team with a dedicated space to examine how they worked together during the Sprint and to identify opportunities for improvement. Unlike the Review, which focuses on product, the Retrospective focuses on process, team dynamics, and communication. It is here that psychological safety becomes particularly important. For a Retrospective to yield honest insights, team members must feel safe to share failures, frustrations, and interpersonal challenges. When this safety exists, the Retrospective becomes a powerful catalyst for trust, because it demonstrates that issues can be discussed openly and addressed constructively.

Together, these events form a feedback-rich communication loop that drives transparency, alignment, and continuous improvement. They also create predictable opportunities for team members to engage with one another, recalibrate their efforts, and reinforce shared goals. When facilitated with intention and supported by a trust-based culture, Scrum events are communicative rituals that underpin effective collaboration.

Importantly, these events are only as effective as the communication behaviours within them. Mechanistic participation, like checking boxes or providing surface-level updates, undermines the purpose of Scrum. Conversely, when teams embrace these events as authentic opportunities to communicate honestly, learn from each other, and adapt together, they become the heartbeat of a high-performing Agile environment.

At the end of the day, Scrum events provide structure for open communication, but it is the team's willingness to engage with them transparently, reflectively, and respectfully that makes them truly impactful. Through regular, structured, and psychologically safe dialogue, Scrum teams enhance delivery, but they also they deepen trust, accountability, and cohesion.

5.9 Barriers to Open Communication

Despite Scrum's emphasis on transparency and frequent feedback, teams often encounter persistent barriers that inhibit truly open communication. These barriers are rarely about technical limitations or tools alone. Frequently they reflect deeper cultural, interpersonal, and organisational dynamics that shape how team members interact and share information.

5.9.1 Psychological Risk

One significant barrier is psychological risk. When individuals fear that speaking candidly might lead to criticism, embarrassment, or damage to their reputation, they are less likely to admit mistakes, voice concerns, or challenge assumptions. This fear can be subtle but pervasive, discouraging the kinds of open, honest exchanges that are essential for problem-solving and continuous improvement.

5.9.2 Hierarchical Residue

Hierarchical residue is another common obstacle. Even in organisations that have embraced Agile frameworks, legacy power dynamics often persist. Team members may hesitate to question decisions, offer dissenting views, or admit uncertainty if they perceive that doing so could conflict with authority or organisational norms. This dynamic reinforces guarded communication and undermines self-organisation.

5.9.3 Fear of Judgement

Fear of judgment also plays a powerful role. Team members may worry about appearing incompetent or unprepared if they disclose gaps in their knowledge or ask for help. This fear can lead to surface-level discussions where genuine issues remain unspoken, resulting in a false sense of alignment that collapses under pressure.

5.9.4 Deference

Deference or cultural silence can compound these barriers, especially in diverse or distributed teams. Different cultural backgrounds may shape how comfortable people feel with directness, disagreement, or admitting mistakes. For some, deference to authority or group harmony is a strong cultural norm, leading to withheld opinions or silent agreement even when reservations exist.

These barriers have tangible consequences for team performance. When communication is constrained:

- Decision latency increases because issues are not surfaced early or resolved collaboratively.
- Knowledge hoarding becomes more likely, as individuals hold back critical information for self- protection or due to lack of trust.
- Performative agility emerges where teams go through the motions of Scrum events without genuine dialogue, undermining adaptation and learning.

Overcoming these barriers requires more than procedural changes. It demands cultivating a climate of psychological safety where vulnerability is accepted and rewarded, actively challenging hierarchical mindsets that stifle participation, and fostering inclusive norms that make space for diverse communication styles. By confronting these obstacles directly, teams can transform superficial rituals into meaningful practices that enable trust, collaboration, and real agility.

5.10 Enablers of Open Communication

While significant barriers can inhibit open communication in Scrum teams, there are also identifiable conditions and practices that actively enable it. These enablers are not superficial techniques but deeply cultural and behavioural foundations that allow teams to share ideas, surface problems, and make collective decisions with confidence:

- A climate of psychological safety is perhaps the most fundamental enabler. When team members believe they can speak up without fear of ridicule, punishment, or damaging their reputation, they are more willing to share uncertainties, admit mistakes, and raise difficult questions. This safety is cultivated through consistent, supportive responses to vulnerability and a shared commitment to treating failures as opportunities for learning rather than blame.
- Trust itself is a reinforcing enabler. When team members observe consistent honesty, follow-through on commitments, and respectful handling of disagreement, they develop confidence in one another's intentions and reliability. This trust lowers the cost of communication, making it easier to ask for help, give feedback, or challenge assumptions without fear of negative consequences.
- Peer modelling of vulnerability is another key enabler. When respected team members, leaders, or Scrum Masters openly admit what they don't know, seek feedback, or own their mistakes, they signal that such behaviours are acceptable and valued. This modelling encourages others to follow suit, establishing norms of openness and mutual support.

- A strong feedback culture is also critical. Regular, timely, and respectful feedback, both formal and informal, keeps communication channels open and expectations aligned. Scrum's ceremonies offer structured opportunities for this (Daily Scrum, Sprint Review, Retrospective), but effective teams supplement these with everyday habits of checking in, clarifying, and offering constructive feedback.
- Transparent leadership practices enable open communication at the organisational level. Leaders who share information freely, explain the reasoning behind decisions, and invite input, demonstrate that openness is valued. Importantly, they also listen actively and respond without defensiveness, reinforcing a sense that all voices matter.
- Additionally, inclusive team norms that honour diverse communication styles and encourage equitable participation help overcome cultural silences or deference. When teams explicitly value different perspectives and make space for all members to contribute, they reduce the risk of hidden disagreement or passive compliance.

These enablers do not arise by accident. They must be cultivated deliberately through team agreements, leadership behaviour, coaching, and continuous reflection. By investing in them, Scrum teams can move beyond mechanical adherence to ceremonies and instead create genuinely collaborative environments where open communication drives trust, learning, and sustained high performance.

5.11 High-Trust vs. Low-Trust Communication Patterns

Understanding the difference between high-trust and low-trust communication patterns is critical for Scrum teams seeking to build truly collaborative environments. These patterns are not simply about what is said, but how communication is structured, received, and acted upon.

In high-trust teams, communication is characterised by transparency and shared ownership. Team members freely share progress updates, surface risks early, and openly admit when they are blocked or need help. Retrospectives are candid and reflective, with participants feeling safe to discuss not only technical issues but also interpersonal dynamics. Disagreements are seen as normal and even productive, as they drive better collective understanding and decision-making. There is a shared mental model of goals, roles, and expectations, reducing duplication and misalignment.

High-trust teams also display active listening and mutual respect. Team members engage attentively, paraphrase to check understanding, and acknowledge diverse perspectives. This creates a strong foundation for adaptive coordination, as people feel heard and valued, making them more willing to share critical insights or raise concerns.

In contrast, low-trust teams often exhibit guarded, transactional communication. Updates may become superficial or self-protective, with individuals emphasising completed tasks while avoiding mention of blockers or uncertainties. Feedback sessions risk being perfunctory, with little meaningful reflection. Retrospectives may avoid sensitive topics, settling instead for safe, surface-level discussions.

Low-trust communication is also marked by role silos and blame-avoidance. Team members may withhold information to maintain personal control or avoid exposing mistakes. Knowledge hoarding can arise out of fear of being seen as less competent or losing perceived advantage. When conflicts do surface, they may be personalised or avoided altogether, leading to unresolved tensions that undermine cohesion and effectiveness.

These patterns have real consequences. High-trust teams adapt more quickly, coordinate more effectively, and innovate more reliably because their communication is open, timely, and grounded in shared purpose. Low-trust teams, by contrast, suffer decision delays, misunderstandings, and fragmented knowledge that reduce their ability to deliver value and respond to change.

Recognising these contrasting patterns allows teams to reflect honestly on their own communication norms. By identifying signs of guarded or siloed communication, deliberate steps can be taken to build trust, transparency can be reinforced, and the collaborative behaviours that underpin high-performing Agile teams can be cultivated.

5.12 Concluding Remarks

In today's fast-paced and interdependent software development environment, trust is a necessity for high-performing Agile teams. Throughout this chapter, it has become clear that trust in Scrum teams is actively built and sustained through open communication which needs to be deeply rooted in both the team culture and the operational structure of Scrum.

Although it may be seen as a process requirement or interpersonal nicety, open communication is a foundational condition that enables transparency, coordination, and psychological safety. Teams that engage in open, honest, and timely communication are more capable of aligning around shared goals, surfacing problems early, and navigating complexity with confidence. This kind of interaction reduces ambiguity and fosters a shared understanding that supports effective, collaborative work.

Yet despite Scrum's emphasis on transparency and frequent feedback, teams often encounter persistent barriers that inhibit truly open communication. These barriers are rarely about tools alone; they reflect deeper cultural, interpersonal, and organisational dynamics. Psychological risk can discourage candour when individuals fear criticism or reputational damage. Hierarchical residue i.e. where persistent legacy power dynamics exist, can make team members hesitate to question decisions or admit uncertainty. Fear of judgment often results in surface-level discussions where genuine issues remain unspoken. Cultural silence or deference can further limit openness, especially in diverse or distributed teams where norms about authority or harmony vary. The consequences are tangible: decision latency, knowledge hoarding, and performative agility that mimics collaboration without enabling it.

Overcoming these barriers requires cultivating a climate of psychological safety where vulnerability is accepted and rewarded, actively challenging hierarchical mindsets that stifle participation, and fostering inclusive norms that make space for diverse communication styles. By confronting these obstacles directly, teams can transform superficial rituals into meaningful practices that enable trust, collaboration, and real agility.

At the same time, there are clear enablers that support open communication. A climate of psychological safety is fundamental; team members must believe they can speak up without fear of ridicule or punishment. Trust itself reinforces openness when people observe consistent honesty, follow-through, and respectful handling of disagreement. Peer modelling of vulnerability where leaders and team members admit mistakes or uncertainties, normalises candid exchange. A strong feedback culture, both formal and informal, keeps channels open and expectations aligned. Transparent leadership practices that invite input and share reasoning reinforce that openness is valued. Inclusive team norms that respect diverse communication styles ensure that all voices are heard.

These enablers do not arise by accident. They are cultivated deliberately through leadership behaviour, team agreements, coaching, and continuous reflection. By investing in them, Scrum teams can move beyond mechanical adherence to ceremonies and create genuinely collaborative environments where open communication drives trust, learning, and sustained high performance.

The difference between high-trust and low-trust communication patterns is stark. High-trust teams communicate with transparency and shared ownership. They share progress updates candidly, surface risks early, and feel safe admitting mistakes. Retrospectives are honest and reflective, and disagreements are welcomed as opportunities for shared understanding. Active listening and mutual respect create adaptive coordination. In contrast, low-trust teams exhibit guarded, transactional communication. Updates are superficial, blockers are hidden, and feedback becomes perfunctory. Role silos and blame-avoidance dominate, with knowledge hoarding and unresolved tensions undermining effectiveness. Recognising these patterns helps teams diagnose their own dynamics and deliberately shift toward behaviours that support trust and collaboration.

Feedback loops are central to sustaining transparency and continuous improvement. Scrum events such as Sprint Reviews and Retrospectives institutionalise reflection and adjustment, creating a rhythm of openness that allows teams to grow and adapt together. When feedback is given and received constructively, it not only drives improvement but reinforces interpersonal trust and shared ownership of outcomes.

Key values such as honesty, integrity, and psychological safety serve as the moral and relational core of trust-based communication. These values are expressed not only in what team members say, but in how they act, viz. by keeping commitments, being forthright, and supporting others even under pressure. When these behaviours are consistently present, they foster a resilient team environment in which openness is both expected and safe.

Scrum's formal events provide the structural opportunities for this communication to occur. Yet their value lies not in the format alone, but in the quality of the interactions they support. When team members participate with authenticity, respect, and a shared commitment to learning, these events become powerful mechanisms for reinforcing trust and cohesion.

Ultimately, open communication is the mechanism through which trust is built, sustained, and operationalised within Scrum teams. Organisations that cultivate this culture, through leadership behaviour, team norms, and structural supports, equip their Agile teams to deliver high-quality outcomes and do so in ways that are adaptive, human-centred, and sustainable over time.

References

McHugh, O., Conboy, K., & Lang, M. (2011). Agile practices: The impact on trust in software project teams. *IEEE Software, 29*(3), 71–76.

O'Connell, T., & Molloy, O. (2018). The antecedents and feedback loops contributing to trust in agile scrum teams. *SOFTENG, 2018*, 16–23.

O'Connell, T. (2019). *A constructivist grounded theory study of the enablers and development of trust in scrum teams* (Doctoral dissertation, NUI Galway).

Schein, E. H. (2010). *Organizational culture and leadership* (Vol. 2). John Wiley & Sons.

Chapter 6
Team Players Versus Individual Contributors

Abstract Agile software development thrives on a deliberate tension: valuing individual excellence while demanding deep collective accountability. Far from being accidental, this dynamic is designed to replace hero-driven productivity with cross-functional collaboration rooted in trust. This chapter examines how Agile reframes individual brilliance as a vital resource embedded in shared goals and mutual respect. It explores how trust, open communication, and psychological safety enable teams to align diverse expertise without sacrificing autonomy, avoiding dysfunction and dominance while sustaining high performance. By tracing Agile's shift from siloed specialisation to integrated, self-organising teams, the chapter shows how practices such as collective accountability, distributed leadership, and peer-based recognition turn personal strengths into a shared asset. Ultimately, it argues that Agile maturity lies in transforming individual potential into collective success i.e. cultivating a culture where the "I" is not lost but elevated through the "we."

6.1 Introduction

Agile software development presents a compelling paradox: it relies on the technical excellence and initiative of individual contributors while demanding deep interdependence and shared accountability across teams. Far from being accidental, this tension is both structural and intentional. Agile frameworks such as Scrum challenge traditional performance paradigms by shifting the emphasis from isolated productivity to collective responsibility, from individual heroism to team coherence. Yet, the question remains: *how can teams preserve and nurture individual excellence without undermining group cohesion?*

This chapter explores that very tension. It contends that Agile does not ask individuals to diminish their unique contributions; rather, it repositions those contributions within a broader, trust-based ecosystem where value is co-created. Drawing on both empirical insights and theoretical foundations, the chapter unpacks how trust, open communication, and psychological safety allow Agile teams to harness the power of individual expertise without devolving into dominance or dysfunction.

T. O'Connell, *Trust in Agile Teams*,
SpringerBriefs in Computer Science, https://doi.org/10.1007/978-3-032-21963-3_6

The chapter begins by tracing Agile's departure from traditional 'hero developer' models toward cross-functional collaboration. It then examines the role of trust in enabling individuals to align with team goals without sacrificing autonomy. Subsequent sections explore how individual excellence becomes a shared asset rather than a structural risk; how collective accountability redefines responsibility; how open communication mediates the autonomy-alignment balance; and how leadership, recognition, and role evolution unfold in non-hierarchical settings. The chapter concludes with a strategic analysis of how teams and organisations can design for both individual and collective success with a final reflection on the cultural shift required to move from "I" to "we," without losing either.

6.2 Revisiting the Agile Manifesto: Individuals and Interactions

Since its publication in 2001, the Agile Manifesto (Beck et al., 2001) has served as a touchstone for teams and organisations seeking more adaptive, collaborative approaches to software development. Among its most quoted values is the emphasis on *"individuals and interactions over processes and tools."* While often cited, this principle is sometimes misunderstood as privileging individual autonomy. In practice, however, it calls attention not to individualism, but to the relational fabric of team success.

Agile was never intended to elevate solo contributors above collective effort. Rather, it recognises that innovation emerges from interaction, viz. through conversations, negotiations, mutual learning, and shared decisions. The focus on individuals is inseparable from their context of collaboration. This chapter argues that high-performing Agile teams honour individual excellence not by isolating it, but by embedding it in structures of trust, open communication, and mutual accountability.

Seen in this light, the Manifesto's values are not diminished but deepened through practices that integrate the "*I*" into a dynamic, interdependent "*we*." As Agile evolves, its founding principles continue to guide not just how software is delivered, but how people work together to co-create value.

6.3 Reframing Individualism in Agile Teams

One of the most persistent tensions in contemporary Agile practice arises from the paradox of valuing individual technical excellence while simultaneously nurturing team cohesion. Agile software development thrives on the creativity, initiative, and expertise of skilled individuals. Yet, it also demands that such talent be exercised in service of collective goals, shared accountability, and continuous collaboration. This dual imperative. i.e. honouring the contributions of high-performing individuals without disrupting the integrity of the team, represents a subtle but critical challenge in Agile environments.

Historically, the software industry valorised the 'hero developer': a lone figure capable of producing exceptional output, often working in isolation and wielding disproportionate influence over project trajectories. While such figures remain mythologised in some organisational cultures, Agile represents a deliberate reorientation away from this archetype. Frameworks such as Scrum emphasise cross-functional teamwork, collective ownership of outcomes, and sustainable development practices that de-emphasise individual glory in favour of collaborative success. The Agile Manifesto itself signals this shift with its emphasis on *"individuals and interactions over processes and tools"* not as an elevation of the lone coder, but as a call to human-centred, co-creative work.

In practice, this recalibration plays out through nuanced interpersonal dynamics within Agile teams. While individuals are often recognised for their distinctive competencies, whether these be technical, analytical, or communicative, such recognition tends to be framed through the lens of team contribution. Practitioners describe environments where mutual respect, psychological safety, and peer validation replace hierarchical recognition structures. Rather than competing for visibility, individuals build trust by delivering reliably, supporting others, and communicating transparently. This reframed individualism, embedded within collaborative norms, appears central to sustaining high-performing Agile teams over time.

6.4 Beyond Specialist Silos: Redefining Collaboration

Traditional software development methodologies such as Waterfall were built around the separation of labour into functionally distinct silos. Analysts would document requirements, designers would develop system architecture, developers would code, and testers would verify functionality. Most often there would be minimal overlap or feedback between roles. This compartmentalisation, while orderly in theory, led to significant inefficiencies in practice: bottlenecks emerged at handoff points, knowledge gaps widened, and accountability became fragmented. The specialist silo model, though technically structured, proved brittle in the face of change, impeding both responsiveness and innovation.

Agile methodologies emerged, in part, as a response to this rigidity. Central to this shift is the cross-functional team, a cohesive unit comprising individuals with diverse, but complementary, skillsets capable of delivering end-to-end value. In frameworks like Scrum, cross-functionality is a structural principle designed to enhance delivery speed, resilience to change, and collective problem-solving. When team members possess overlapping competencies and shared accountability, work can flow more continuously and adaptively. Dependencies on external specialists are reduced, and teams become more self-sufficient in responding to shifting priorities or emergent issues.

However, transitioning from siloed roles to cross-functional collaboration represents a profound cultural transformation. In the Agile teams, this transition demands a reorientation from individual ownership of tasks to shared responsibility for outcomes. Developers and testers, for example, must learn to engage in ongoing dialogue rather than sequential handoffs; analysts can and should feel comfortable, contributing to technical discussions beyond the requirements phase. This cultural adaptation, moving from a mindset of 'my contribution' to 'our outcome' is facilitated by practices that encourage knowledge sharing, role fluidity, and mutual learning. Yet, this adaptation can also surface latent tensions, particularly where legacy role identities or hierarchical habits persisted. Cross-functionality is a dynamic capability that teams must cultivate deliberately over time. It is not a static attribute.

6.5 The Role of Trust in Balancing Autonomy and Alignment

In agile software development, the challenge of sustaining both individual autonomy and team alignment is fundamentally relational. This balance hinges on trust which is the critical enabler that allows high-performing individuals to defer to the needs of the collective without compromising their own professional identity or intrinsic motivation. Rather than perceiving alignment as a threat to autonomy, team members in high-trust environments understand it as a shared commitment to purpose. Trust thus becomes the mechanism through which individuals voluntarily recalibrate their personal goals in service of a greater whole.

The mitigation of ego-driven behaviour is central to this process. In the absence of trust, skilled contributors may feel compelled to assert their technical dominance or defend their domain expertise, often at the expense of cohesion. However, where trust is present and actively cultivated, through open communication, psychological safety, and demonstrated respect, such impulses are tempered. Mutual respect is a prerequisite for deferring to others' decisions, particularly in cross-functional teams where expertise is distributed. Trust, in this sense, does not dissolve individual identities; rather, it dignifies them within a collective framework. It enables members to recognise the legitimacy of others' contributions and to situate their own within a larger, integrative tapestry of work.

This dynamic gives rise to what Boreham (2004) and others have termed *collective competence*, i.e. a state in which the team's functional intelligence and adaptability exceed the capabilities of any single member. Collective competence is not a passive aggregation of skills, but an emergent property of collaboration underpinned by trust. It reflects a form of distributed cognition wherein roles are fluid, knowledge is shared, and decision-making becomes a negotiated process grounded in mutual accountability. Such competence is not sustained by rigid coordination mechanisms, rather it is perpetuated by trust-based interactions that allow for flexible adaptation to emergent challenges.

Thus, trust is not merely a social nicety in Agile teams; it is the scaffolding upon which autonomy and alignment can coexist. It fosters a professional ethos where individual excellence is amplified by collective engagement.

6.6 Individual Excellence as a Resource, not a Risk

Agile teams thrive on the principle that every member brings unique value. This can be through technical expertise, domain knowledge, or creative insight. However, the presence of individual brilliance is not inherently beneficial; it becomes an asset only when integrated into the team's collective functioning. High-trust teams are distinguished by their ability to absorb individual excellence in ways that enhance, rather than destabilise, group cohesion.

In low-trust environments, unintegrated excellence often manifests as dysfunction. It would not be uncommon for 'rock star' developers to dominate conversations, resist critique, or withhold knowledge as a means of preserving status. These behaviours, though sometimes rationalised as necessary for velocity or innovation, ultimately undermine psychological safety and reduce the group's willingness to engage in open collaboration. The hoarding of knowledge, in particular, is frequently acknowledged as a barrier to learning and adaptability, which are known to be two cornerstones of Agile responsiveness.

In contrast, teams with a strong foundation of interpersonal trust manage to channel high-performing individuals into roles of constructive influence rather than control. Expertise is respected but not idolised. Decision-making remains a collaborative process, with individual contributions being recognised in proportion to the task at hand, not the persona of the contributor. This reflects what could be described as a 'non-hierarchical respect,' i.e. an environment where competence earns authority, but never at the expense of mutual regard or shared accountability.

Thus, trust acts as a buffer against the concentration of influence. In high-trust teams, no single individual is permitted to eclipse the collective voice. Instead, the group develops mechanisms, which are often informal but robust, for integrating expertise without compromising cohesion. This includes practices such as rotating facilitation roles, deliberate inclusion of quieter voices, and reflective retrospectives where the team critically examines its own dynamics.

Crucially, this orientation reframes individual excellence not as a threat to be managed, but as a resource to be harmonised. Trust enables teams to harness brilliance without breeding dependency, fragility, or division. In doing so, they embody the Agile ideal: adaptive, self-organising units where the whole is genuinely greater than the sum of its parts.

6.7 Collective Accountability: The Structural Shift in Scrum

Scrum represents a deliberate structural departure from traditional models of software development, where accountability is typically tied to individual task ownership. In conventional environments, responsibility is siloed, i.e. developers are assigned discrete deliverables, and success is measured in terms of personal output. However, Agile frameworks like Scrum reconfigure this paradigm through the mechanism of collective accountability, embodied most clearly in the concept of the Sprint Goal.

As opposed to being a compilation of individual to-do lists, the Sprint Goal is a shared commitment to a coherent outcome. While tasks may be distributed among team members based on expertise or availability, the accountability for achieving the goal is mutual. This reframing requires a significant cultural shift: team members must begin to see their contributions not as isolated efforts but as interdependent actions in pursuit of a collective objective. Effectively, 'It's not about what *I* did, it's about what *we* delivered.'

Scrum ceremonies operationalise this shift by redistributing responsibility at key junctures of the development cycle. Sprint Planning transforms what might otherwise be a managerial directive into a co-constructed plan, fostering alignment and shared ownership from the outset. Similarly, Retrospectives are not post-mortems for individual performance; they are structured opportunities for the team to collectively examine its processes, decision-making, and interpersonal dynamics. This ritualised reflection reinforces the team's accountability not just for *what* is delivered, but *how* it was achieved.

These practices reveal that high-trust Scrum teams distribute authority and responsibility in ways that support both cohesion and autonomy. They do not merely divide labour. The team commits together, reflects together, and learns together. Importantly, this shared accountability does not erase individual agency. Rather, it situates personal contributions within a larger narrative of team success, where responsibility is not diluted but diffused intelligently across the group.

In this way, Scrum fosters a mature, interdependent form of accountability. It is accountability that transcends blame and incentivises continuous learning. It aligns structural mechanisms with the social realities of trust, enabling teams to operate with both rigor and resilience in complex, fast-moving environments.

6.8 Open Communication as the Mediator

In Agile teams, open communication plays a pivotal role in enabling collaboration, sustaining trust, and balancing the needs of the individual with those of the collective. Open communication refers to a team culture of transparency, curiosity, and reciprocal listening i.e.one that allows diverse perspectives to contribute meaningfully to shared goals without undermining cohesion. It is more than just the routine exchange of updates or status reports.

This communicative openness is inextricably linked to psychological safety. Individuals feel they can speak up, admit mistakes, and challenge ideas without fear of ridicule or marginalisation. When team members feel safe to express uncertainty or disagreement, they are more likely to surface issues and risks early, propose creative alternatives, and engage in constructive critique. Such environments value dissent as a catalyst for learning and improvement.

Importantly, open communication is what allows teams to benefit from individual insights without becoming fragmented by them. In teams where communication norms support respectful dialogue, disagreement is perceived as a necessary component of intelligent decision-making. It is not seen as a threat to group harmony. Agile ceremonies such as Sprint Planning and Retrospectives create deliberate opportunities for this kind of exchange, fostering a culture where reflective dialogue is not the exception but the expectation.

High-performing teams distinguish themselves by maintaining a team-first mindset while actively making space for the individual voice. Members are encouraged to bring their full expertise to the table, knowing that their contributions will be considered in context and not in isolation. This balance ensures that no single viewpoint dominates, while also avoiding the pitfalls of groupthink or passive conformity.

Ultimately, open communication acts as the mediator between autonomy and alignment. It ensures that trust is not assumed but practiced, and that collaboration is not coerced but chosen by the team members. In doing so, it transforms the team into a dynamic, adaptive unit where shared goals are enriched by the unique perspectives of its members.

6.9 The "We" of Collaboration

Agile team working is far more than cooperative task execution, it is the dynamic construction of a shared identity, a collective "*we*" that emerges through ongoing interaction. This "we" is not a slogan or a management ideal; it is a lived experience grounded in mutual trust, psychological safety, and co-ownership of outcomes. When Agile teams succeed, it is not because they eliminate individual differences, but because they find ways to align those differences in pursuit of a common goal.

In this context, the team becomes a collaborative system of meaning-making and problem-solving. Practices such as Daily Stand-ups, Sprint Planning and Retrospectives, do more than just coordinate work, they cultivate shared mental models and a sense of collective efficacy. The "we" is continually negotiated and reinforced through open communication, inclusive decision-making, and peer-based recognition.

Understanding Agile teamwork as the collaborative *'we'* offers a useful lens for interpreting many of the dynamics discussed in this chapter. It emphasises that collaboration in Agile is not passive alignment, but active engagement in a social system designed to elevate individual contributions through relational cohesion. It is this collaborative "we" that enables teams to adapt, learn, and perform in complex, evolving environments.

6.10 Leadership, Recognition, and Role Evolution

Agile teams challenge conventional notions of leadership by decoupling influence from formal authority. Rather than relying on fixed hierarchies or designated roles to direct team activity, Agile environments foster *distributed leadership*. This is a dynamic in which individuals step forward based on contextual relevance, domain expertise, or initiative. Leadership becomes situational and fluid, not positional. This shift is foundational to the adaptability and responsiveness of high-performing teams.

In practice, this means that decision-making is not monopolised by seniority but shared in a manner that reflects the collective intelligence of the group. A developer with deep system knowledge may lead technical design discussions; a tester may take ownership of release coordination; a less experienced team member may drive innovation by asking incisive, clarifying questions. Teams come to recognise that leadership in Agile is not about control, rather it is about contribution, and about knowing when to lead and when to follow.

This model of distributed leadership raises important questions around recognition. Without formal titles or hierarchical structures, how do Agile teams acknowledge and reward individual excellence? The answer lies in a redefinition of recognition itself. In well-functioning Agile teams, recognition is peer-based and embedded in the day-to-day rhythm of collaboration. It is expressed through the visible impact of one's contributions on team goals, as opposed to through individual performance metrics or appraisal rankings. When a team member unblocks a critical issue, offers timely support, or introduces a process improvement, that act is immediately felt and informally affirmed by peers.

Recognition, given when it is authentic, context-sensitive, and immediate is more meaningful to team members than traditional performance evaluation mechanisms. It affirms a team member's value within the team while reinforcing shared ownership of outcomes. Moreover, it allows roles to evolve organically over time. As trust deepens and team members gain confidence, individuals often expand their responsibilities, take on mentoring functions, or assume temporary leadership in emergent situations. This evolution is not assigned from management, but negotiated in the team through interaction, reflection, and mutual respect.

In this way, Agile teams cultivate a model of leadership that is both distributed and developmental. Recognition becomes a cultural practice that sustains morale, reinforces trust, and encourages continuous growth. By avoiding rigid hierarchies, Agile teams preserve their adaptability while still honouring the distinct contributions that make high performance possible.

6.11 Strategic Implications for Individual and Team Success

The cultivation of trust within Agile teams has important strategic implications for how organisations design, support, and evaluate team performance. Rather than favouring either individual brilliance or collective conformity, high-performing Agile teams demonstrate that sustainable success arises from integrating the two. To enable this integration, intentional design decisions must be made at the levels of team composition, coaching, and measurement.

Team design must move beyond simplistic dichotomies of "generalist versus specialist." Instead, the most resilient teams maintain a deliberate blend of deep expertise and broad capability. Specialists bring depth in key technical domains, ensuring architectural integrity and domain insight. Generalists contribute flexibility, adaptability, and cross-functional awareness, which are particularly vital in iterative environments where scope can evolve rapidly. The strategic challenge is to create a team ecosystem where individual strengths are leveraged without creating single points of failure. This requires structures that promote both autonomy and interdependence, allowing members to stretch beyond their core competencies through collaboration and cross-training.

Coaching strategies also play a vital role in supporting this balance. High performers can elevate team performance, but only when integrated thoughtfully. Effective Agile coaching involves relational stewardship more than skills facilitation. It is important to ensure that exceptional individuals contribute without fostering dependency, ego-driven dynamics, or bottlenecks. Coaches and Scrum Masters must remain alert to early signals of imbalance, such as deferred decision-making or overreliance on specific individuals, and intervene with practices that promote distributed knowledge and shared leadership. Rotating roles, and knowledge-sharing sessions are practical tools that reinforce collective ownership while preserving individual excellence.

Measurement frameworks must likewise evolve to reflect the relational and adaptive nature of Agile work. Traditional performance metrics which are focused on individual output, task completion, or isolated productivity, often fail to capture the health or effectiveness of the team as a unit. In contrast, team-oriented metrics such as sprint velocity, shared code ownership, and the distribution of work across skillsets offer a more holistic view of performance. Additionally, indicators like peer feedback, participation in retrospectives, and involvement in mentoring or cross-training initiatives provide qualitative insight into team cohesion and knowledge flow.

Ultimately, designing for both individual and team success demands a cultural mindset grounded in trust, mutual respect, and a shared sense of purpose. When organisations align their practices with these principles, they create the conditions in which both individual potential and collective capability can flourish.

6.12 Conclusion: From "I" to "We" .... Without Losing Either

Agile practice, at its best, is not a rejection of individual excellence. It does not diminish the value of personal skill, insight, or initiative; rather, it situates these attributes within a broader commitment to collective success. The shift from "I" to "we" in Agile teams is not about erasure of the self; in fact, it is about elevation through integration. In high-performing teams, individuals contribute to a shared endeavour where their strengths are recognised, valued, and multiplied through collaboration.

Maintaining this delicate balance requires more than adherence to methods and structures. It is sustained through the invisible infrastructure of trust, open communication, and psychological safety. These foundational qualities allow team members to take risks, defer to others, and receive feedback without defensiveness. Open communication ensures that diverse perspectives are not only heard but constructively engaged. Psychological safety creates the conditions under which disagreement becomes productive, and growth becomes mutual. Together, these elements form the relational fabric that enables autonomy and alignment to coexist.

The strategic insight here is both simple and profound: the most effective Agile teams are not composed of the brightest individuals working in parallel, they are made up of people who know how to bring out the best in each other. Excellence, in this context, becomes a shared resource rather than a competitive asset. It is distributed, amplified, and sustained through relationships of trust.

As Agile continues to evolve in response to growing complexity and rapid change, organisations must resist the temptation to revert to individualised performance models or hierarchical leadership as proxies for control. Instead, organisations should design and support environments in which individuals can excel *through* their teams and not despite them. In doing so, they will cultivate not only higher-performing teams, but healthier, more human ways of working.

6.13 Concluding Remarks

The challenge of balancing individual excellence with collective accountability lies at the heart of Agile practice. As this chapter has demonstrated, high-performing Agile teams do not resolve this tension by favouring one over the other. Instead, they create the conditions in which both can thrive. This can best occur through trust, open communication, distributed leadership, and shared responsibility.

Agile frameworks intentionally move away from traditional models that celebrate individual heroism, replacing them with structures that support interdependence and mutual recognition. Yet this is not a turn toward conformity or the erasure of individual distinction. On the contrary, Agile teams succeed when they deliberately integrate diverse strengths, enabling individuals to contribute meaningfully while remaining deeply accountable to the collective.

Key to this integration is a cultural foundation that values psychological safety, peer-based recognition, and situational leadership. These elements allow teams to absorb high performers without becoming dependent on them, and to distribute ownership in a way that is flexible, equitable, and resilient. Metrics shift accordingly, from evaluating isolated outputs to assessing team-level effectiveness, adaptability, and learning capacity.

Ultimately, this chapter has argued that Agile maturity is not measured solely by process adherence or delivery speed, but by a team's ability to transform individual potential into shared success. The most effective Agile teams are more than collections of competent individuals; they are collaborative systems that amplify excellence through connection. In moving from individualism to interdependence, they do not lose the "I", rather they elevate it through the "we."

References

Beck, K., Beedle, M., Van Bennekum, A., Cockburn, A., Cunningham, W., Fowler, M.,... & Thomas, D. (2001). Manifesto for agile software development.

Boreham, N. (2004). A theory of collective competence: Challenging the neo-liberal individualisation of performance at work. *British Journal of Educational Studies, 52*(1), 5–17.

Chapter 7
Developing a Strong Team Ethos

Abstract Agile teams are often recognised for their speed and adaptability, but their true strength lies in something deeper: a shared team ethos. This chapter explores how team ethos, defined as the collective values, relational habits, and cultural norms that shape how teams work together to act as the invisible engine of Agile success. Drawing on insights from practice and theory, it reveals how shared values, distributed ownership, and mutual trust turn frameworks like Scrum into lived, resilient collaboration. From rituals and onboarding to conflict navigation and cultural diversity, the chapter shows that high-performing teams are not just aligned in tasks but connected in purpose. It argues that team ethos is a structural necessity, enabling cohesion, adaptability, and psychological safety. As Agile becomes increasingly global and virtual, the intentional cultivation and repair of ethos become essential. This is not about harmony or perfection but about fostering the conditions where people can collaborate authentically, take collective ownership, and grow together. Agile teams may deliver in code, but they thrive in culture, and it is their ethos that makes them endure.

7.1 Introduction

Agile teams are often celebrated for their velocity, adaptability, and ability to deliver working software. But behind every successful sprint, every smooth handoff, and every moment of creative collaboration lies something deeper and less visible: the *team ethos*. This ethos which can be described as the shared spirit, values, and relational fabric that hold a team together, is not captured in any backlog or burn-down chart. Yet without it, Agile frameworks risk becoming mechanical and superficial.

In Agile environments a strong team ethos is the cultural operating system that enables the technical one to function. It shapes how trust is built, how conflict is resolved, how individuals contribute, and how ownership is distributed. Teams that thrive are not just aligned on *what* they are doing: they are committed to *how* they are doing it, and to *who* they are doing it with.

T. O'Connell, *Trust in Agile Teams*,
SpringerBriefs in Computer Science, https://doi.org/10.1007/978-3-032-21963-3_7

This chapter explores the architecture of that ethos. It looks beyond process and output to the human foundations of Agile success: the shared values that give teams direction, the ownership practices that foster accountability, and the interpersonal dynamics that turn cooperation into cohesion. This chapter will explore how stories, rituals, and symbols reinforce belonging, and how culture is preserved and repaired in moments of transition, conflict, or change.

In a world of cross-functional, distributed, and culturally diverse teams, building a team ethos is not just about working well, it's about *working well together*. What follows is both a reflection and hopefully a guide: an exploration of the conditions that help Agile teams do more than deliver. These are the conditions that help Agile teams *endure, adapt, and grow.*

7.2 What is a Team Ethos?

A well-managed backlog or a clearly defined Sprint Goal is at the heart of every high-performing Agile team What distinguishes truly effective teams is something less tangible but profoundly influential: a shared team ethos. This ethos represents the collective spirit, values, and behavioural norms that bind team members together. Hierarchy or obligation are not involved, rather the team becomes cohesive through mutual respect, trust, and a sense of belonging. It is what enables teams to function as more than the sum of their parts, shaping how individuals relate to one another, how they make decisions, and how they navigate challenges over time.

Team ethos is not codified in tools or captured in process documentation; it is embedded in *how* the team works together. It is reflected in unspoken agreements about quality, collaboration, and support. It is felt in the way conflicts are addressed, feedback is offered, and success is celebrated. While goals, tasks, and roles may shift from sprint to sprint, a strong team ethos provides continuity, i.e. a shared cultural baseline that holds the team together across uncertainty and change.

In Agile contexts, cultivating a team ethos is a prerequisite for Agile maturity. Frameworks like Scrum are often adopted as structural interventions, but their success depends largely on social conditions. Without a strong relational foundation, even the most disciplined application of ceremonies, roles, and artefacts will fall short. Agile maturity is not defined just by velocity or predictability, it is expressed in how well teams embody values such as openness, courage, commitment, and respect in their daily practice.

This emphasis on human dynamics is woven into the Agile Manifesto (Beck et al., 2001), whose first value prioritises "*individuals and interactions over processes and tools.*" While sometimes misread as a call for individual autonomy, this principle is more accurately understood as a call to relational awareness. Agile does not ask teams to abandon structure, but to root their practices in meaningful interaction. Trust and shared accountability are the scaffolding on which effective Agile teams are built. Teams that thrive are those that move beyond mere cooperation to genuine cohesion, where members feel safe to speak, commit to collective goals, and defer to one another's expertise without fear of reprisal or being judged.

This chapter explores how such a team ethos is cultivated and sustained. It considers the interpersonal, structural, and cultural elements that help Agile teams not just deliver together but *belong* together. In doing so, it offers a roadmap for developing a relational foundation robust enough to support autonomy, accountability, and enduring collaboration.

7.3 From Shared Goals to Shared Values

It is one thing for a team to share a goal; it is another altogether to share values. In many Agile teams, particularly those in fast-paced delivery environments, there is a strong emphasis on meeting deadlines, completing backlogs, and achieving measurable outcomes. While these shared goals are essential for alignment and progress, they are not sufficient to sustain a healthy, resilient team over time. For a team to function as a cohesive unit, not just a group of individuals working in parallel, it must also develop a shared set of values that guide behaviour, decision-making, and interpersonal relationships.

Shared goals describe *what* the team is trying to achieve; shared values shape *how* the team works together to get there. They encompass principles such as trust, respect, openness, and accountability. These values are not imposed from the outside, nor are they captured fully in mission statements or onboarding presentations. Instead, they emerge gradually: most usually through conversation, collaboration, and the cumulative effect of day-to-day actions. When a team chooses to listen to each other with respect, supports a colleague in difficulty, or admits a mistake without fear, it is living its values.

The distinction between a *work group* and a *team* lies in this very difference. Work groups often consist of individuals working alongside each other, perhaps toward a common objective, but each accountable primarily for their own piece of the puzzle (Zayed & Kamel, 2005). In contrast, a team is characterised by mutual reliance, shared responsibility, and a commitment to collective success (Katzenbach & Smith, 2008). It is the difference between simply dividing up the work and owning the outcome together (Bisbey & Salas, 2019).

Developing shared values is a deeply social process. It doesn't happen in one meeting or through a checklist. Instead, it grows in moments of challenge, for example, when timelines slip, when disagreements arise, when feedback must be given and received. It is in these moments that a team's values are revealed, tested, and either reinforced or eroded.

Agile frameworks, particularly Scrum, create the space for values to emerge and evolve. Ceremonies like Sprint Planning, Retrospectives, and Daily Standups are more than project management routines; they are cultural rituals that promote transparency, empathy, and learning. These rituals invite team members to speak honestly, reflect on their performance, and re-commit to each other as well as the work. In doing so, they cultivate a sense of shared purpose that transcends any single task or role.

However, shared values are not identical values. Agile teams are often diverse in skills, experiences, and working styles. The goal is not to erase individuality but to create a common ground, a core of mutual understanding and respect from which collaboration can thrive. This requires intentional effort: articulating what matters to the team, revisiting those commitments regularly, and embedding them in daily interactions.

When teams operate from shared values, they become communities of trust and accountability, i.e. places where people not only perform, but also grow. Shared values are the invisible architecture of team cohesion. Without them, collaboration remains fragile and transactional. With them, it becomes sustainable, meaningful, and transformative.

7.4 Ownership as a Cultural Practice

In Agile environments, ownership is a cultural stance that defines how team members relate to the work, to each other, and to the outcomes they produce together. While traditional models of accountability often emphasise personal responsibility within functionally siloed roles, Agile teams approach ownership as a shared commitment to collective delivery. This shift represents a cultural transformation that reshapes how success and responsibility are understood and enacted.

In many conventional work groups, individuals are assigned tasks by a manager and held accountable for their personal performance. The assumption is that strong leadership, clear task division, and individual productivity will lead to overall project success. But this model does not reflect the fluid, interdependent nature of Agile teamwork, where uncertainty, change, and iteration are the norm. Instead, Agile teams succeed when ownership is distributed, i.e. when all members feel equally responsible for the team's goals, outcomes, and ongoing improvement.

This ethos is deeply embedded in the Scrum framework. The Sprint Planning meeting, for example, marks a key moment of shared commitment: the team does not merely receive instructions but collectively decides what work they will take on and how they will achieve it. In doing so, they co-author the Sprint Goal and take joint responsibility for its delivery. Unlike in a work group where individuals are accountable only for their own tasks, Scrum teams hold each other mutually accountable for the success of the Sprint as a whole.

Daily Standups and Retrospectives reinforce this sense of shared ownership. In the Daily Standup, team members report not to a manager but to one another, providing visibility into progress, surfacing impediments, and making collaborative adjustments. Retrospectives provide a regular space to reflect on *how* the team is working, not just *what* it is delivering. In these spaces, ownership extends beyond deliverables to include the team's dynamics, values, and learning.

Importantly, shared ownership does not mean role ambiguity or a loss of individual agency. Rather, it invites individuals to step into responsibility proactively, offer help across boundaries, and contribute beyond formal definitions of their roles. This often takes the form of informal mentoring, knowledge sharing, or stepping up during a crisis, not because one is told to, but because it is what the team needs.

The culture of ownership is especially visible in how teams handle problems. In high-accountability teams, a blocker or issue affecting one person is seen as everyone's concern. Team members do not isolate failure or blame. Instead, they collaborate to resolve the issue by shifting tasks, reallocating effort, or rethinking the approach. The mindset becomes one of shared consequence because if the sprint fails, we *all* fail. If it succeeds, it is because of *our* effort, not just the heroics of a few.

Over time, this distributed ownership fosters a team environment that is more resilient, adaptive, and self-correcting. It also encourages a higher standard of engagement. Individuals do not just execute tasks, they care about the work, about their teammates, and about the quality of the outcomes they produce together.

In this way, ownership in Agile teams evolves from a managerial construct into a cultural practice which is embedded in rituals, reinforced through trust, and enacted through shared responsibility. It is this transformation that allows Agile teams not only to move fast, but to move *together*.

7.5 Cohesion Through Trust and Respect

Team cohesion is often misunderstood as uniformity or constant agreement. In high-functioning Agile teams, however, it is trust and respect that allow conflict to be navigated constructively. Cohesion is not the absence of conflict, it is the invisible force that holds a team together through ambiguity, challenge, and change. This does not occur through obligation or hierarchy, but through mutual belief in one another's intent, integrity, and contribution.

Agile frameworks implicitly rely on this cohesion. Unlike traditional project teams that may defer decisions to a project manager or escalate tensions up a chain of command, Agile teams are designed to be self-organising. This design assumes a level of psychological maturity and interpersonal trust: individuals can voice concerns, share responsibility, and depend on one another to act in the best interest of the team. Without this foundation, self-organisation falters into chaos or reverts to informal hierarchy.

Although delivering on commitments matters, trust is not simply about reliability. It also involves interpersonal risk-taking, i.e. the ability to admit mistakes, ask for help, raise doubts, and challenge ideas without fear of embarrassment or retaliation. Respect, in turn, means recognising the value of each team member's expertise and perspective, even, or especially, when it differs from our own. Together, trust and respect create a climate in which open communication thrives, and team members feel empowered to contribute authentically.

Cohesion in Agile teams is also fostered through interdependence. When team members rely on each other not just to coordinate work, but to complete tasks collaboratively, they must develop shared understanding, mutual support, and ongoing alignment. This is visible in practices like pair programming, test-and-code integration, or collaborative story refinement, where shared ownership of both problems and solutions is the norm.

Importantly, cohesion is not static. It deepens over time through repeated experiences of dependability, fairness, and constructive dialogue. Team rituals such as Retrospectives play a key role in this process by offering regular opportunities to reflect on team dynamics, resolve tensions, and strengthen the group's relational fabric. These moments of honest conversation build both alignment and affiliation i.e. a sense that "we are in this together."

However, cohesion should never come at the expense of silence or conformity. When teams mistake cohesion for harmony, they risk suppressing dissent or excluding alternative perspectives. The goal is not agreement for its own sake, but a sense of collective unity with space for individual voices. Teams that strike this balance are those that grow stronger through disagreement.

Ultimately, trust and respect are structural necessities of Agile teams They enable a level of collaboration that cannot be mandated, only earned. And in environments where iteration is fast, complexity is high, and solutions must be co-created, cohesion becomes the catalyst for both performance and well-being.

7.6 Rituals, Symbols, and Stories

Every strong team culture is underpinned not only by shared values but by the rituals, symbols, and stories that give those values form and expression. These elements, often overlooked in technical discussions of Agile practice, play a crucial role in reinforcing team identity, creating psychological safety, and embedding a sense of continuity and belonging. They provide the emotional and cultural scaffolding that supports trust, collaboration, and long-term cohesion.

In Agile teams, rituals are functional and symbolic, i.e. they are not just ceremonial. Scrum events such as Sprint Planning, Daily Standups, Reviews, and Retrospectives serve practical purposes: aligning on goals, sharing progress, and identifying blockers. But they also do much more. These rituals establish rhythms, set expectations for engagement, and offer structured opportunities for reflection and renewal. When practiced consistently, they help teams develop a shared cadence, a sense of forward motion in which everyone participates.

Beyond formal Scrum events, many teams develop their own informal rituals: kicking off each week with a "Monday kick-off," ending Sprints with celebratory demos, or holding informal "show and tell" sessions. Some teams start Standups with a quick round of personal check-ins or finish them with a team cheer. These practices, while seemingly trivial, serve an important purpose, in that they humanise the work, reinforce community, and signal that the team is more than a set of tasks.

Symbols, too, play a role in shaping team ethos. These may be literal, such as kanban boards, shared emojis, team mascots, or workspace artefacts, or more abstract, such as nicknames for projects or insider terminology. Over time, these symbols become shorthand for shared meaning. A physical task board filled with coloured sticky notes isn't just a planning tool; it becomes a visual representation of progress, effort, and shared achievement. Likewise, a team Slack channel filled with gifs and inside jokes may seem frivolous, but it signals psychological safety and peer connection.

Perhaps most powerfully, teams develop stories or narratives about who they are, what they've overcome, and how they work together. These stories might be about the Sprint where everything went wrong and the team pulled together to recover. Or the launch that was nearly derailed, but a last-minute collaboration turned things around. Stories encode shared learning and identity. They allow teams to look back with pride, laugh at past struggles, and carry forward a sense of capability. Over time, they form the team's informal oral history which functions as a powerful source of continuity, especially in the face of change.

These cultural elements are not static or superficial. They evolve as the team evolves, and they can be intentionally shaped. Leaders and Scrum Masters can cultivate rituals that promote inclusion and growth, encourage storytelling in Retrospectives, or amplify positive symbols that reinforce team values. More importantly, teams themselves can co-create these practices, generating traditions that feel authentic rather than imposed.

When rituals, symbols, and stories are aligned with a team's values, they help transform abstract principles into lived experiences. They provide moments of pause and connection in fast-paced environments. More importantly, they contribute to a culture where people feel seen, trusted, and part of something larger than themselves.

7.7 Sustaining Ethos Through Onboarding

A team ethos, once established, is not self-sustaining. One of the most vulnerable moments for any Agile team is the introduction of a new member. While onboarding is often treated as a technical or procedural task which is focused on tools, systems, and workflow access, it also represents a critical cultural inflection point. How a team welcomes and integrates a new colleague can either reinforce its ethos or allow it to erode.

New members arrive with their own norms, assumptions, and expectations about collaboration. If left unacknowledged, these differences may create friction, misalignment, or even silence, particularly if the team relies on informal practices or tacit understandings that are difficult for outsiders to interpret. For this reason, high-functioning teams treat onboarding as a relational process of cultural invitation. Transmission of knowledge can follow once this has occurred.

Effective cultural onboarding involves more than formal briefings. It includes storytelling, i.e. sharing the team's history, key rituals, values-in-practice, and pivotal moments of growth. Practices such as pairing new members with experienced team "buddies," involving them in Retrospectives from the outset, or taking time to narrate decisions and informal norms during meetings all help surface the invisible architecture of team life. In addition to orienting the new team member, these gestures reaffirm the team's collective identity.

Importantly, onboarding is reciprocal. New members bring fresh perspectives, and thoughtful teams remain open to learning from them. Asking new colleagues what they notice, what feels unfamiliar, or how their previous experiences compare can offer valuable insight and prevent the solidification of unhelpful group habits. This openness preserves ethos while allowing it to evolve.

Ultimately, sustaining a strong team ethos requires that every new beginning is treated with intentionality. By integrating people, not just into the workflow, but into the cultural life of the team, Agile teams reinforce belonging, accelerate cohesion, and protect the very foundation that enables effective collaboration.

7.8 Adapting Team Ethos Across Cultures and Remote Contexts

As Agile teams become increasingly global and distributed, the cultivation of a strong team ethos must be reimagined for cultural diversity and virtual collaboration. While the core ingredients of ethos, i.e. shared values, mutual trust, and psychological safety, remain constant, the ways in which they are expressed, reinforced, and experienced can vary significantly depending on cultural norms and the nature of remote work.

In co-located teams, ethos is often shaped through spontaneous, informal interaction. This can include conversations over coffee, impromptu whiteboard sessions, or the non-verbal cues of shared physical space. In distributed or hybrid teams, these organic touchpoints are less accessible, making it necessary to deliberately engineer moments of connection and cohesion. Virtual standups, Retrospectives, and Sprint planning meetings become not just coordination tools but essential cultural rituals, where tone, inclusion, and relational presence must be consciously cultivated.

Cultural variation adds further complexity. Norms around hierarchy, feedback, conflict, and humour differ across regions and backgrounds. For example, direct critique may be valued as honesty in one culture and perceived as disrespect in another. Silence might indicate reflection in some contexts, disengagement in others. Without awareness of these dynamics, well-intentioned practices may inadvertently damage trust or reduce psychological safety.

High-performing Agile teams address this by developing an awareness of cultural difference and embedding inclusive practices into their routines. This may include clarifying communication preferences, rotating facilitation roles to balance voices, or explicitly discussing how team values such as respect and openness are interpreted by different members. Agile coaches and Scrum Masters play a key role here by fostering dialogue that surfaces assumptions and encourages mutual learning.

Digital collaboration tools also carry symbolic weight in remote teams. Emojis, reaction icons, custom workflows, or even background images in video calls can become part of the team's cultural grammar. These micro-symbols help express tone, build rapport, and reinforce a sense of shared identity in the absence of physical proximity.

Crucially, remote and multicultural teams benefit from intentionally designed rituals of belonging. These might include non-task touchpoints, such as virtual coffee chats, team storytelling sessions, or asynchronous check-ins that invite emotional presence. Such moments humanise the work and keep the relational core of the team alive.

In essence, a strong team ethos requires a high degree of adaptation. It is not limited by geography or background. Agile values can serve as a universal starting point, but they must be translated into culturally sensitive, contextually relevant practices. When teams approach this translation with humility, curiosity, and commitment, they enrich it through diversity.

7.9 The Fragility and Repair of Team Ethos

A strong team ethos can take months to build, but it can take only minutes to fracture. While shared values, rituals, and trust provide a foundation for collaboration, this foundation is not immune to stress. In fact, one of the most important, and often overlooked aspects of team culture is not how it is built, but how it is maintained and repaired when it is tested.

Team ethos is inherently fragile because it depends on relational dynamics, viz. trust, respect, shared understanding, and psychological safety. These elements are cultivated through consistent, positive interactions. However, they can be quickly eroded by breakdowns in communication, unaddressed conflict, perceived unfairness, or failures in accountability. When team members no longer feel safe to speak up, or when contributions go unrecognised, the shared sense of "*we*" begins to weaken.

Agile teams are particularly exposed to this fragility because they work in high-change, high-visibility environments. Tight deadlines, unclear expectations, or shifts in leadership can unsettle team dynamics. Even small lapses such as missed commitments, disrespectful comments, or passive disengagement, can accumulate and begin to disrupt the cultural fabric. And because Agile teams are designed to be self-managing, there may be no external authority to step in and repair the damage.

That is why repair is as essential to team culture as initial formation. It is not that high-performing teams never falter, rather they are the ones that know how to recover. Repair involves naming the tension, revisiting shared commitments, and re-establishing trust through action. Agile frameworks provide natural entry points for this work: the Retrospective, for example, is a space specifically designed to surface breakdowns and co-create solutions. When used authentically, the Retrospective becomes an opportunity to pause, reflect, and realign. In effect, it serves as a renewal and recalibration for the team.

However, repair depends on interpersonal courage. It requires team members to speak honestly about discomfort, offer and receive feedback, and take responsibility for their impact. It demands humility, empathy, and a belief that improvement is possible in relationships within the team.

Leaders play a critical role in modelling and supporting this repair process. By responding non-defensively to feedback, naming issues without blame, and reinforcing shared values, they help create a climate in which honesty is safe, and learning is prioritised over perfection. But in a truly resilient team, the responsibility for repair is shared. Everyone contributes to the emotional maintenance of the team, in the same way as they do to its technical work.

The ability to repair ethos is what transforms Agile teams into adaptive systems. It is what allows teams to grow through difficulty, rather than being undone by it. And it reinforces the understanding that culture is a living system that must be tended, revisited, and renewed.

7.10 Strategic Implications for Leaders and Coaches

Developing and sustaining a strong team ethos is not the exclusive responsibility of any one person, but leaders and Agile coaches play a vital enabling role. Their influence is not exerted through command-and-control authority, but through the cultivation of environments where shared values, ownership, and cohesion can take root and thrive. This requires a shift in focus, from managing tasks to stewarding culture.

First and foremost, leaders must model the ethos they want to see. Values such as openness, respect, and accountability are made visible in how leaders respond to uncertainty, how they handle disagreement, and how they treat others when mistakes occur. Leaders who ask for feedback, admit when they're wrong, and celebrate collective wins reinforce psychological safety and mutual trust. This modelling sends a powerful signal: *in this team, how we treat each other matters*.

Agile coaches and Scrum Masters, in particular, are well-placed to act as culture facilitators. They help make the invisible visible by surfacing team dynamics, challenging unhelpful patterns, and guiding conversations that strengthen team identity. Rather than solving problems on behalf of the team, they build capability within the team to handle issues together. This includes supporting conflict resolution, encouraging inclusive dialogue, and reinforcing team rituals that anchor shared values.

One strategic implication is the importance of intentional team design. Rather than focusing solely on technical skills, team formation should consider interpersonal compatibility, diversity of perspectives, and readiness to collaborate. Bringing together people with complementary strengths, both technical and interpersonal, lays the groundwork for a cohesive, adaptive unit. Leaders must also ensure that teams are given the autonomy to self-organise, while providing enough support and structure to prevent fragmentation.

Measurement is another key area of consideration. Traditional performance indicators often reward individual output, reinforcing siloed behaviour. Instead, leaders should shift toward team-oriented metrics that reflect collaboration, shared accountability, and learning. Examples include team velocity, participation in Retrospectives, cross-skilling efforts, and qualitative feedback on team climate. What gets measured signals what is valued, and teams will respond accordingly.

Finally, leaders must accept that team ethos cannot be mandated. It is co-created through consistent investment in relationships, rituals, and reflection. This means making time for culture work: celebrating team stories, running diversity workshops and embedding moments of connection into everyday routines.

When leaders and coaches take culture as seriously as delivery, they create teams that are both productive and deeply engaged, i.e. teams that adapt under pressure, support one another through difficulty, and take pride in the way they work, not just what they deliver. In short, they help teams become more than the sum of their parts by leading with intention, humility, and care.

7.11 Conclusion: Building More Than Code

Agile teams are often measured by their velocity, throughput, or ability to deliver value early and often. But beneath these surface indicators lies something far more enduring and impactful: the team's ethos. This ethos which encompasses the shared values, norms, and relational habits that define how a team works together, is what sustains performance, especially when challenges arise. It is the difference between a group of people who complete tasks and a team that co-creates, adapts, and grows.

This chapter has explored how a strong team ethos is built not just on shared goals, but on shared values, mutual ownership, and deep interpersonal cohesion. It is enacted daily through rituals, stories, and collaboration. However, just as importantly, it must be repaired when strained. These cultural practices are the structural foundations that make agility possible.

Leaders, coaches, and team members all play a role in shaping and sustaining this ethos. It is not enough to have the right processes in place; what matters is how those processes are lived. Agile ceremonies, for example, become powerful only when trust, respect, and psychological safety are present. Similarly, self-organisation works only when people feel empowered and committed to one another's success.

In the end, the most successful Agile teams are not those with the best tools or the most polished processes. They are the teams where people listen before they act, care as much about each other as they do about the work and hold themselves accountable. This accountability extends beyond output and includes how they show up together. These are the teams that build more than software. They build resilience, meaning, and trust.

To build a strong team ethos is to invest not only in delivery, but in the long-term health, adaptability, and humanity of the team. Agile teams may be measured in code, but they thrive in culture.

7.12 Concluding Remarks

As this chapter has discussed, the strength of an Agile team lies in far more than its technical competence or process discipline. The true strength of an Agile team lies in the quality of its shared ethos, i.e. the web of values, norms, and relationships that shape how people work together. In high-functioning teams, ethos is not a decorative ideal. It is the living culture that sustains agility through change, complexity, and challenge.

This ethos is built through deliberate investment in shared values, distributed ownership, and interpersonal cohesion. It takes root in rituals and stories, gains strength through trust and respect, and finds continuity even amid turnover through thoughtful onboarding. It is tested by tension and disruption and proven through a team's capacity to repair and realign. Whether a team is co-located or remote, culturally uniform or globally distributed, a strong ethos offers both a compass and a connective tissue.

A strong team ethos is not a fixed achievement but a continual practice. As Agile teams evolve, so too must their cultural foundations. Leadership, therefore, becomes an act of stewardship: enabling conditions for belonging, listening for signs of fragility, and modelling the values that the team aspires to embody.

In the end, team ethos is not about agreement or perfection. It is about creating an environment where people feel safe to show up, contribute meaningfully, and navigate the work together with shared purpose. Agile teams may be measured by code committed, velocity achieved, or features delivered, but what truly distinguishes the best among them is how they treat each other, and how they rise together.

To develop a strong team ethos is to lay the groundwork for productivity, but also for trust, resilience, and sustainable collaboration. It is what turns Agile from a method into a lived experience. And it is what makes great teams not just possible but enduring.

References

Beck, K., Beedle, M., Van Bennekum, A., Cockburn, A., Cunningham, W., Fowler, M.,... & Thomas, D. (2001). Manifesto for agile software development.

Bisbey, T. M., & Salas, E. (2019). Team dynamics and processes in the workplace. In *Oxford research encyclopedia of psychology*.

Katzenbach, J. R., & Smith, D. K. (2008). *The discipline of teams*. Harvard Business Press.

Zayed, A. M., & Kamel, M. M. (2005). *Teams and work groups*. Cario University.

Chapter 8
Collaboration, Knowledge Sharing, and Psychological Safety

Abstract Agile teams succeed through process but also through how they relate, learn, and grow together. This chapter explores the critical shift from transactional communication to genuine collaboration, where knowledge is actively shared, trust forms the basis of team interaction, and psychological safety is a necessary condition rather than an optional ideal. Drawing on research, team practice, and lived experience, it examines how effective collaboration goes beyond coordination to become a process of co-creation. Agile teams that thrive do more than follow rituals and use tools. They embed trust into their day-to-day routines, their decisions, and their feedback practices. They treat knowledge as a collective asset, built through openness, reflection, and mutual respect. The chapter identifies collaboration patterns and anti-patterns, explores the role of leadership in fostering safety, and presents practical strategies for designing teams that prioritise learning, inclusion, and resilience. High-performing Agile teams are technically competent. They are intentional in how they work together. Collaboration is not a supplementary activity. It is the core of how Agile teams learn, adapt, and succeed. When collaboration is done well, Agile teams build software. But they also build capability, cohesion, and shared intelligence.

8.1 Introduction

Agile teams thrive or fail by how they work together. While Stand-ups, Backlogs, and Scrum boards are visible artefacts of Agile delivery, the true differentiator of high-performing teams lies deeper. It is in how they connect, learn, and evolve together. This chapter explores that deeper layer: the transition from basic communication to genuine collaboration, where knowledge becomes a shared resource, trust becomes an operational backbone, and psychological safety is no longer optional but essential.

In many teams, collaboration is conflated with communication. Calendars are full, updates are constant, and messages stream endlessly. Yet beneath this flurry of interaction, true collaboration may be absent. Collaboration is not merely the exchange of information, rather it is the co-creation of meaning, insight, and direction; it is "actively working together to deliver a work product or make a decision" according

T. O'Connell, *Trust in Agile Teams*,
SpringerBriefs in Computer Science, https://doi.org/10.1007/978-3-032-21963-3_8

to Cockburn and Highsmith (2002). It is what allows a team to become more than the sum of its parts: beyond well-coordinated, but instead, truly cohesive, adaptive, and resilient.

In Agile contexts, this matters profoundly. Agile practices assume technical excellence but also social interdependence. They presuppose that individuals can challenge, support, and learn from one another without fear. Without this, rituals become rote, tools become superficial, and learning slows. Teams may deliver, but they do not grow.

This chapter asks a critical question: *What does it take for Agile teams to move beyond communication and into collaboration that is safe, sustainable, and strategic?*

Drawing from research, grounded practice, and lived team experience, the conditions under which knowledge truly flows will be explored. How trust, mindset, tooling, and leadership combine to shape collaborative dynamics and team capability will also be described.

As the chapter unfolds, both theory and practice will be encountered, from the psychological scaffolding of collaboration to the visible patterns and anti-patterns of team life, and to the strategic design choices that embed learning into everyday work. The aim is to illuminate what good collaboration looks like, but also to equip teams and leaders to cultivate it intentionally.

What follows is a journey into the social architecture of agility with an ever-present reminder, that, in Agile, people, as opposed to being their roles, are also learners, co-creators, and custodians of shared knowledge. When they collaborate well, they build better teams as well as better products.

8.2 From Communication to Collaboration

In Agile environments, collaboration is the connective tissue that sustains learning, innovation, and adaptability. While communication is foundational, collaboration represents a deeper, more active mode of engagement: it is the difference between exchanging information and creating shared meaning. It is a shift in mindset from coordination to co-creation, where the goal is insight, innovation, and team capability.

This chapter begins by exploring the critical shift from transactional communication to trust-based collaboration, where knowledge is cultivated collectively. Agile frameworks like Scrum, XP, and SAFe presume a level of interdependence that cannot be sustained without psychological safety. Teams that work in isolation, even those that use Agile rituals, may meet delivery targets but fail to achieve cohesion, innovation, or long-term resilience. True collaboration emerges when individuals feel safe enough to ask questions, challenge assumptions, admit uncertainty, and learn out loud.

Safe knowledge flow, then, is a deliberate outcome of team culture, design, and trust. It demands not only technical integration but perhaps more importantly, emotional permission i.e. the assurance that speaking up will not incur social risk, that experimentation is valued, and that learning is a collective act rather than a personal burden.

This is especially relevant in knowledge-rich environments where the rapid pace of change demands both execution and also reflection. In such contexts, learning is continuous, and knowledge is often tacit, i.e. being expressed in dialogue as opposed to in documents. Therefore, Agile teams must design for collaboration as both a cultural practice and an architectural priority. Teams must not only ask, "*Are we communicating enough?*" but also, "*Are we learning together in a way that enhances our collective capability*?".

At the core of this dynamic lies the connection between collaboration, learning, and resilience. Agile teams that collaborate deeply are better equipped to respond to change, solve novel problems, and grow stronger through adversity. In contrast, teams that communicate without truly collaborating may meet short-term goals, but they forfeit the adaptive capacity that defines long-term success.

In the sections that follow, the social and structural conditions that support knowledge-sharing collaboration will be explored. These include not only team culture and trust, but also the tools, rituals, and mindset shifts that make learning visible and safe. The goal is to equip Agile practitioners with practical strategies for cultivating collaboration, not as an ideal, but as an everyday practice essential to agility.

8.3 Psychological Safety and Collaborative Practice

Psychological safety, which describes the shared belief that a team environment is safe for interpersonal risk-taking, is a foundational condition for effective collaboration in Agile teams. In the absence of this safety, individuals may withhold questions, conceal mistakes, or avoid challenging assumptions, thereby stifling the open exchange of knowledge. Teams that lack psychological safety may still deliver work, but they do so without the interpersonal depth required for learning, adaptation, and resilience.

In psychologically safe teams, by contrast, vulnerability is normalised. Team members can ask for help, offer dissenting opinions, or admit uncertainty without fearing judgment or reprisals. This climate of openness fosters mutual trust and encourages active participation, making it possible for knowledge to flow freely across roles, levels of experience, and technical boundaries.

Agile practices like pair programming and mob programming are powerful precisely because they depend on knowledge sharing and collaboration whilst also reinforcing psychological safety. In pair programming, two developers work closely together, continually discussing decisions, reasoning, and code. This creates not just technical quality but also shared understanding. When team members feel secure in questioning one another, they learn faster, challenge assumptions more effectively, and build a culture of reciprocal accountability.

Mob programming, in which the entire team collaborates on a task in real time, makes this process even more collective. It transforms problem-solving into a public, participatory activity. When practiced in psychologically safe environments, mobbing allows for real-time learning, distributed decision-making, and the emergence of shared mental models. Knowledge is not siloed in individuals but becomes visible, testable, and co-constructed.

The same principles apply to shared Retrospectives, which provide regular opportunities for teams to pause, reflect, and adapt. In high-trust environments, Retrospectives become moments of cultural renewal. Teams can name tensions, celebrate progress, and negotiate improvements without defensiveness. When team members feel safe to speak candidly, Retrospectives generate not just insight but alignment and cohesion.

In all of these practices, psychological safety acts as an enabling force. It allows individuals to bring their full cognitive and emotional presence into collaborative spaces. As safety deepens, so too does the team's capacity for shared ownership, creative problem-solving, and continuous improvement.

Ultimately, collaboration in Agile teams is a cultural achievement. It emerges when individuals feel respected, heard, and empowered to contribute. Investing in psychological safety is the condition that makes collaboration, and the knowledge sharing it requires possible. Ultimately it leads to Agile success.

8.4 Practical Markers of Unsafe Versus Safe Teams

While trust is often discussed in abstract or philosophical terms, its presence, or absence, can be observed in the day-to-day rhythms of Agile team life. Certain behaviours serve as practical markers, illuminating whether a team operates in an environment of psychological safety or navigates the undercurrents of distrust and fear.

In teams where psychological safety is diminished, Retrospectives tend to become performative rituals rather than meaningful forums for reflection. Members may respond with prolonged silence, offering superficial observations or avoiding controversial topics altogether. The language used during Sprint reviews or defect discussions may reveal subtle patterns of blame: phrases like "*Who broke this?*" or "*Why didn't you catch that?*" reflect a culture where error is penalised rather than examined. Avoidance behaviours also proliferate. Developers may resist pair programming, testers may disengage from planning sessions, and junior members might remain passive in decision-making, fearing negative evaluation.

In contrast, teams marked by high psychological safety exhibit visible and frequent help-seeking behaviours. Developers readily ask for assistance or clarification without concern for appearing incompetent. Feedback is offered constructively and received without defensiveness, allowing for continuous learning and adaptive growth. Problem-solving becomes a collaborative endeavour, with team members co-owning both challenges and solutions. Importantly, dissenting views are welcomed as critical inputs to team learning.

A case vignette may serve to illustrate this distinction: In an Agile team, a production outage caused by a misconfigured deployment script led to a tense retrospective. The Scrum Master initiated the session by asking, "*Who ran the deployment?*", immediately narrowing the conversation to fault-finding. The room fell silent. One developer quietly admitted responsibility, prompting a defensive exchange and visible discomfort. In a different team facing a similar incident, the retrospective began with the question, "*What did our process miss that allowed this to happen?*" This alternative framing encouraged open dialogue, during which multiple team members contributed insights into testing gaps, communication lapses, and automation blind spots. The outcome was a shared commitment to refine deployment protocols, not assign blame.

8.5 Knowledge Sharing as a Cultural and Structural Practice

In high-performing Agile teams, knowledge sharing is not a peripheral activity confined to wikis or Sprint documentation. It is a continuous relational process embedded in both culture and structure. This dynamic exchange of insights and experiences enables collective intelligence to emerge, adapt, and endure beyond the contributions of any single team member.

At its core, knowledge sharing is less about the storage of artefacts and more about the flow of meaning across social connections. Practices such as pair programming and mobbing exemplify this fluidity, transforming coding from an individual task into a co-creative act. In these settings, team members actively transmit tacit knowledge, and this can be through such means as debugging strategies, architectural reasoning, coding idioms, through dialogue, observation, and joint problem-solving. Similarly, informal practices like "brown bag" sessions or "show-and-tells" foster cross-pollination of ideas, particularly in environments where interdisciplinary collaboration is valued. Internal demos provide a public space for teams to not only showcase completed features but also surface design trade-offs, implementation challenges, and lessons learned. This serves to institutionalise reflection.

Conversely, knowledge hoarding, whether this is deliberate or inadvertent, poses a silent threat to team cohesion and resilience. Individuals who centralise expertise, control key parts of the code, or fail to externalise their decision-making processes create informational bottlenecks. While such behaviours may emerge from time constraints, role ambiguity, or perceived job security concerns, the result is the same: a fragile team structure overdependent on a few knowledge holders. This undermines Agile principles of shared ownership and adaptability, leaving teams vulnerable to knowledge loss through turnover or burnout.

Crucially, the most effective teams treat knowledge sharing as a recurring practice that both reflects and reinforces trust. Structural mechanisms (e.g., rotation of responsibilities, backlog grooming in cross-functional groups) align with cultural signals (e.g., openness to questions, valuing exploratory conversations) to create a learning ecosystem. In such environments, team members are active contributors to a living, shared body of knowledge that sustains both delivery and development as opposed to mere repositories of information.

These contrasting examples underscore the tangible manifestations of trust, or its erosion, in Agile teams. Identifying such markers not only aids leaders in diagnosing team climate but also offers a roadmap for cultivating healthier, more resilient team cultures.

8.6 Collaboration Patterns and Anti-Patterns

Effective collaboration is a cornerstone of Agile practice, yet its quality varies significantly across teams. Collaboration involves intentional, trust-rich interactions that support shared ownership, knowledge flow, and mutual accountability. While Agile frameworks promote practices that facilitate collaboration, their success depends on how they are enacted in context. Certain patterns reliably foster cohesion and adaptive problem-solving, while others, which are often adopted unintentionally, can erode trust, entrench silos, and reduce the team's collective effectiveness. Understanding these patterns is essential for developing healthy team dynamics and sustaining high performance.

8.6.1 Patterns that Foster Collaboration

To build and sustain trust, Agile teams rely on a set of well-established collaboration practices. These patterns reinforce shared ownership, transparency, and mutual support, all of which are key ingredients of a cohesive and high-functioning team.

8.6.1.1 Pair Programming

Pairing transforms individual coding into a shared cognitive task, enabling real-time feedback, co-learning, and mutual verification. It builds rapport, reduces knowledge silos, and encourages openness to critique. When practiced with psychological safety, pair programming enhances both code quality and interpersonal trust.

8.6.1.2 Peer Reviews

Peer reviews, when positioned as collaborative dialogues rather than evaluative checkpoints, encourage shared responsibility for design and implementation decisions. They provide structured opportunities for knowledge sharing, facilitate the diffusion of best practices, and foster a sense of communal ownership over the codebase.

8.6.1.3 Swarming on Stories

Swarming involves mobilising multiple team members around a single user story or challenge, particularly in response to intractable issues i.e. blockers or urgent priorities. This pattern reflects a team-first mentality, where completing work collectively is valued over preserving individual task allocations. It reinforces alignment, resilience, and cross-functional awareness.

8.6.1.4 Collective Code Ownership

When all team members feel accountable for all parts of the codebase, territorial behaviours diminish and collaboration flourishes. Collective ownership fosters proactivity, reduces bottlenecks, and ensures that technical debt or defects are treated as team-wide concerns, not individual oversights.

While these patterns offer a foundation for effective teamwork, their impact depends on consistent practice and cultural reinforcement. In parallel, teams must remain vigilant to the emergence of counterproductive behaviours that, over time, can erode the very trust these patterns aim to build.

Not all collaboration practices are constructive. Certain recurring behaviours and structures, which can be adopted unintentionally, can undermine trust, fragment knowledge, and weaken team cohesion.

8.6.2 Collaboration Anti-Patterns

Anti-patterns often emerge subtly. They can be shaped by organisational habits, team history, or well-intentioned shortcuts. Left unexamined, they can become normalised, gradually corroding psychological safety and collaborative capacity. What follows are some of the most common collaboration anti-patterns observed in Agile environments.

8.6.2.1 Hero Culture

In some teams, particular individuals are valorised for solving critical problems or delivering under pressure. While seemingly beneficial, this creates dependency structures and implicitly discourages others from taking initiative. It also signals that success is individual, not collective. This is a notion that runs completely counter to Agile principles.

8.6.2.2 Silent Handoffs

Passing work between individuals without meaningful context exchange leads to miscommunication, duplicated effort, and delays. This anti-pattern reduces transparency and erodes the continuity of understanding needed for cohesive team delivery.

8.6.2.3 Knowledge Silos

When expertise is confined to a small subset of individuals, either intentionally or due to unstructured processes, teams become fragile. Silos inhibit learning, slow onboarding, and create single points of failure, particularly when key members are absent or leave the team.

8.6.2.4 Tool Overuse Without Connection

Heavy reliance on digital tools without accompanying interpersonal interaction can reduce collaboration to transactional updates. Tools such as Jira or Slack are valuable for coordination but cannot replace the trust-building and problem-solving that occurs through face-to-face (or synchronous) dialogue. When tools replace, rather than support, human connection, team cohesion suffers.

Understanding these collaboration patterns and anti-patterns equips Agile teams with the awareness needed to reflect on their own practices. More than technique, collaboration is a cultural and relational achievement, which can be sustained through continuous attention to how people work together, not just what they produce.

8.7 Tools that Enable and Tools that Distract

Digital tools are essential to contemporary Agile work. They help coordinate distributed teams, manage complex backlogs, track code changes, and surface important metrics. But the tools themselves are not inherently collaborative. Their value lies in how they are used, i.e. how well they reflect and reinforce team values, and how effectively they support human connection, not replace it. Agile teams that thrive incorporate tools into a culture of trust, shared purpose and responsive communication.

Enabling tools serve as infrastructure for transparency, alignment, and shared ownership. When used mindfully, they extend and amplify collaboration. Version control systems like Git allow multiple developers to co-author code with clarity and accountability, especially when paired with thoughtful branching strategies and peer review practices. Team chat platforms such as Slack or Microsoft Teams can lower the barrier to help-seeking and support fast, lightweight coordination. Whiteboarding tools like Miro or MURAL recreate some of the spatial, creative affordances of in-person brainstorming, particularly valuable for distributed or hybrid teams. Wikis and shared documentation systems centralise knowledge and reduce rework, provided they are actively maintained and collaboratively authored.

The key thread across these tools is not their *functionality* rather it is their *fit*. When tools align with a team's rhythms, rituals, and communication norms, they reinforce trust and shared cognition. A well-used tool doesn't just support workflow; it becomes part of the team's collective memory and identity.

However, Agile teams are also vulnerable to tool overreach. As work becomes increasingly mediated through digital platforms, there is a risk of substituting interaction with instrumentation. Updating tickets, commenting asynchronously, or responding with emoji reactions can create an illusion of alignment. However, these can also conceal confusion, hesitation, or disengagement. When tools are used to *avoid* difficult conversations, they do not enable, instead they insulate.

This over-reliance is particularly visible when tooling drives process rather than supports it. Rigid workflows in tools like Jira or Azure DevOps may box teams into artificial constraints, obscuring the need for conversation, negotiation, and adaptation. Similarly, analytics dashboards and burn-down charts, while useful, can create performative pressure if not interpreted in context. In such environments, tool usage becomes performative rather than relational.

Moreover, tools can unintentionally entrench silos. When documentation or discussions are scattered across multiple platforms, or when access and participation are uneven, some voices are marginalised. This can reinforce knowledge gaps and create invisible hierarchies of expertise or access. These conditions are antithetical to Agile principles of inclusivity and shared ownership.

Ultimately, tools should *extend human trust*, not replace it. The most effective teams regularly interrogate their tooling landscape, asking not just "*Is this working?*" but "*How is this shaping the way we relate, decide, and collaborate?*" A Retrospective dedicated to tool usage, or a periodic "manual Sprint" that reduces digital mediation, can reveal hidden dependencies and open space for more intentional interaction.

Agile is, at its heart, a human practice. Tools that honour that truth, by enhancing dialogue, visibility, and mutual support, are the ones worth keeping.

8.8 Mindset Shifts for Leaders and Teams

Agile collaboration is animated by mindset. The attitudes, assumptions, and reflexes that team members and leaders bring to their work shape how knowledge flows, how safety is experienced, and how decisions are shared. For trust to take root and collaboration to flourish, a fundamental shift in mindset is required: from individual control to collective contribution; from certainty to curiosity; from knowing to learning.

At the core of this shift are several interrelated dispositions: humility, curiosity, transparency, honesty, integrity, and openness. These are not abstract ideals, they are everyday practices that shape how team members relate, engage, and grow together:

- Humility enables individuals to recognise the limits of their perspective and remain open to input from others. In a team context, humility is not self-effacement, rather it is an active recognition that good ideas can come from anywhere, and that strength lies in shared intelligence, not personal infallibility.
- Curiosity fuels inquiry. It encourages team members to ask questions rather than make assumptions, to seek understanding before offering judgment. In high-trust teams, curiosity replaces defensiveness, turning difference into dialogue.
- Transparency closes the loop. It involves sharing not only work artefacts, but also thought processes, uncertainties, and reasoning. Transparency allows others to understand how decisions are made and invites co-ownership of both problems and solutions.
- Honesty and integrity ensure that what is communicated reflects reality. Together they mean owning errors, admitting uncertainty, and speaking truthfully, even when doing so feels uncomfortable. These qualities underpin reliability and psychological safety: when people believe that others are sincere and consistent, trust can take root.
- Openness is both cognitive and emotional. It involves receptiveness to new ideas, feedback, and experiences, as well as the willingness to be seen and heard. Openness makes space for vulnerability and enables deep, reciprocal learning.

Collectively, these mindsets represent a departure from traditional, expert-centric models of software development, where knowledge is concentrated in a few roles and validated through authority. Agile teams that thrive reject this paradigm. They treat knowledge as a team-enabled system, where learning is continuous, distributed, and co-created through interaction. Expertise is still valued, but it is fluid and shareable, not hoarded or gatekept.

The implications for leadership are profound. Leaders in trust-rich Agile environments are facilitators of collective capability. This requires modelling fallibility, not as a weakness, but as an invitation to honesty. When a Scrum Master admits they misunderstood a requirement, or when a Product Owner openly reflects on a missed prioritisation, they create a permission structure for the team to do the same.

Equally important is the ability to invite dissent. Agile leaders must tolerate opposing views. Given there will sometimes be dissent, Agile leaders must *design for this*. This includes structuring meetings to surface diverse perspectives, explicitly soliciting alternative viewpoints, and creating psychological safety for disagreement. Over time, dissent becomes a form of engagement, not rebellion.

Finally, leaders must reward learning. In many environments, output is still celebrated more than insight. Yet the most resilient Agile teams are not those that ship the most features, they are those that learn the fastest. Recognising moments of reflection, acknowledging growth after failure, and celebrating team-wide improvements signal that learning is a valued outcome in its own right.

Mindset shifts are not one-off events. They emerge through practice, reflection, and reinforcement. As teams internalise these values of humility, honesty, curiosity, integrity, transparency, and openness, they enhance collaboration, but more importantly they cultivate a culture in which trust is continually renewed. In such environments, knowledge becomes not just *what* is known, but *how* it is shared and who feels safe enough to share it.

8.9 Trust-Driven Decision-Making in Agile Teams

Decision-making in Agile contexts is a relational act, deeply intertwined with the team's level of psychological safety and trust. How decisions are made, who is involved, and how dissent is handled all signal the health of team dynamics and directly influence delivery outcomes.

In trust-rich teams, decision-making tends to be distributed, transparent, and inclusive. Members feel confident voicing uncertainties or challenging prevailing assumptions, knowing that disagreement is not equated with disloyalty. This fosters better outcomes by mitigating groupthink and surfacing a broader range of perspectives. For example, in high-trust teams, backlog refinement may involve not just the Product Owner and tech leads, but developers, testers, and UX specialists, each contributing domain-specific insight. Decisions around technical trade-offs or estimation are approached collaboratively, with the recognition that collective input leads to more sustainable, informed outcomes.

Conversely, in low-trust environments, decision-making often becomes centralised or opaque. Individuals may defer to dominant voices, avoid challenging flawed assumptions, or remain silent even when critical issues arise. This leads to brittle solutions, role ambiguity, and accountability gaps. Team members may perceive decisions as imposed rather than co-created, eroding ownership and engagement. In such environments, speed often comes at the expense of quality and cohesion.

Importantly, trust does not eliminate conflict, it reshapes it. Healthy disagreement, when handled respectfully, becomes a mechanism for learning and refinement. Teams that trust one another can engage in robust debates about architecture, design, or priorities without escalating into personal conflict. What distinguishes these teams is not a lack of tension, but their ability to navigate tension constructively.

Embedding trust into decision-making processes requires intentional scaffolding: establishing clear decision rights, fostering open dialogue, and creating rituals that invite reflection. Whether through structured consensus-building techniques (e.g. fist-to-five voting, delegation poker) or informal alignment conversations, the goal is to ensure that decisions are made together.

8.10 Autonomy and Alignment: The Dual Engines of Trust

In high-functioning Agile teams, autonomy and alignment are interdependent drivers of trust, performance, and sustainable delivery. Autonomy gives individuals and teams the discretion to act on their expertise, while alignment ensures that such actions cohere with broader goals, values, and constraints. When balanced effectively, these elements create an environment where trust is not only granted but earned and reinforced through consistent, value-driven behaviour.

Autonomy: when grounded in trust, empowers team members to make decisions, experiment, and take ownership of outcomes. Developers who feel trusted are more likely to innovate, surface issues early, and pursue continuous improvement without waiting for permission. Autonomy fosters a sense of intrinsic motivation and personal responsibility, both of which are essential for creative problem-solving and adaptive responsiveness. However, autonomy without alignment can lead to fragmentation, viz. isolated decisions, duplicated work, and divergence from strategic goals.

Alignment: provides the directional clarity that gives autonomy its shape and purpose. It is cultivated through shared vision, frequent communication, and ongoing dialogue about priorities and constraints. In Agile settings, alignment is reinforced through artefacts such as the Product Backlog, Sprint goals, and Definition of Done. However, it is also a cultural achievement. Teams that are aligned operate with a shared sense of what matters and why, enabling faster, more coherent decisions even in the absence of top-down control.

Trust plays a pivotal role in mediating this balance. Leaders who trust their teams do not micromanage, they provide context, clarify intent, and then step back. Teams that trust one another self-organise more effectively, knowing that peers will act in good faith, uphold standards, and surface misalignments early. Conversely, a lack of trust often manifests as over-control, rigid approvals, or delayed decision-making which are symptoms of an organisation that lacks confidence in its own people.

Practices that strengthen the autonomy-alignment dynamic include regular strategy briefings, rotating leadership roles within teams, and feedback loops that connect technical decisions to customer impact. These practices actively reinforce trust by demonstrating that autonomy is respected and alignment is co-created.

8.11 Conflict as a Catalyst: Navigating Tension in Trust-Rich Teams

Conflict in Agile teams is not inherently negative. Instead, conflict is a normal and necessary part of team development. Drawing on Tuckman's influential model (Tuckman, 1965), of group formation i.e. Forming, Storming, Norming, Performing, and Adjourning, conflict should be understood not as a failure of collaboration but as a developmental milestone. In particular, the Storming phase is marked by tension, competing perspectives, and role negotiation. It is here that trust is either forged or fractured, depending on how the team navigates disagreement.

In psychologically safe teams, conflict during the Storming phase is recognised as a rite of passage. It is a chance to surface assumptions, challenge ideas, and negotiate shared values. Teams that embrace this phase rather than rush through it lay the groundwork for genuine cohesion in the Norming and Performing stages. Open disagreement is not just tolerated, it is expected and welcomed. Members feel safe to question architectural decisions, backlog priorities, or delivery commitments, knowing that the team views dissent as an opportunity for collective learning, not personal challenge.

Conversely, when teams suppress or avoid conflict during the Storming phase, trust remains superficial. Passive compliance replaces meaningful dialogue, and unresolved tensions often resurface later as miscommunication, low engagement, or breakdowns in delivery. In these contexts, conflict may be redirected into blame, defensiveness, or covert resistance, which undermines both psychological safety and progress toward high performance.

Trust-rich teams develop specific mechanisms for engaging with conflict constructively. These may include facilitated Retrospectives that explore tension without retribution, collaborative dialogue frameworks such as "ladder of inference" or "disagree and commit," and shared norms that explicitly separate the critique of ideas from a critique of individuals. Importantly, they recognise that conflict doesn't disappear at the Performing stage, it simply becomes more sophisticated, more respectful, and more focused on value creation.

Leaders play a pivotal role throughout Tuckman's stages, particularly by normalising the Storming phase. When leaders model vulnerability, encourage dissent, and frame conflict as a sign of engagement, they help the team metabolise tension into trust. This scaffolding enables the transition from Forming to Performing, not as a linear path, but as an iterative journey punctuated by recalibration.

Ultimately, it is the way in which conflict is handled that determines a team's health. Teams that learn to engage with tension reflectively and respectfully progress more effectively through Tuckman's stages and cultivate a deeper, more resilient form of trust.

8.12 Repairing the Flow When Collaboration Breaks Down

Even in the most cohesive Agile teams, collaboration can falter. Trust may waver, alignment may fray, and participation may recede into silence. When this happens, teams often experience a subtle but cumulative breakdown in what makes Agile work: open dialogue, mutual support, and shared ownership. Rather than viewing these moments as failures, high-functioning teams treat them as signals or indicators that something in the system needs attention. Just as Agile values continuous delivery, it must also embrace continuous repair.

The signs of misalignment or disengagement are often subtle at first:

- Team members stop raising concerns during Retrospectives.
- Conversations become shorter, safer, more scripted.
- Decisions revert to a few dominant voices.
- Individuals silently pick up tasks but rarely collaborate.
- Feedback is withheld or offered in ways that feel guarded or transactional.

These shifts may seem minor, but over time they point to a breakdown in flow. Whilst these shifts can affect the workflow, they can also have a detrimental effect on the relational and cognitive flow, viz. the dynamic exchange of ideas, trust, and mutual energy that fuels collective work. When this flow is blocked, collaboration suffers, and with it, innovation, adaptability, and resilience.

Rather than pushing forward as if nothing is wrong, teams that excel in the long term know how to pause and repair. They create deliberate interventions to reset connection and re-establish shared purpose. Common strategies include:

- **Team Reset Workshops**: these are structured, facilitated sessions that revisit team agreements, roles, and shared values. These workshops provide psychological permission to name tensions, clarify boundaries, and co-design new norms. They are especially valuable after significant change, such as personnel turnover, failed deliveries, or leadership shifts.
- **Open Retrospectives**: open Retrospectives invite reflection on team culture, relational dynamics, and emotional climate. When teams feel safe enough to ask, "*How are we really working together?*", they begin to move beyond symptoms and toward root causes.
- **Facilitated Feedback Loops**: when interpersonal dynamics feel tense or feedback has gone stale, bringing in a neutral facilitator can help reintroduce constructive dialogue. Techniques such as "start/stop/continue," appreciative inquiry, or nonviolent communication frameworks can help depersonalise conflict and reignite mutual respect.

These interventions are most powerful when accompanied by continuous reflection and realignment. Repair is an ongoing process as opposed to a single event. Teams that regularly ask, "*What's working and what's drifting?*" are more likely to maintain coherence under pressure. Reflection does not need to be formal to be effective. It could be as simple as a ten-minute check-in, a one-question pulse survey, or a shared journal of working agreements can all sustain alignment.

Ultimately, breakdowns in collaboration are opportunities. They offer a chance to examine what has been taken for granted, to confront what is unsaid, and to rediscover shared intent. Teams that treat these moments as growth points, as opposed to threats, develop not only better ways of working, but deeper relational capital.

In Agile, flow is more than just velocity. It is the felt sense of moving forward together, with clarity, connection, and care. When that flow breaks down, repair is not a detour. It is the way back to trust.

8.13 Repairing Trust After Breaches

In any team, breaches of trust are inevitable. Deadlines are missed, commitments falter, feedback is mishandled, or interpersonal missteps occur. In high-performing Agile teams, trust is defined by the presence of a repair mechanism as opposed to an absence of failure. What distinguishes resilient teams is that they recognise, address, and recover from breaches of trust in ways that strengthen rather than corrode their cohesion.

Trust breaches often occur in subtle, cumulative ways. A team member may fail to follow through on a task, remain silent during an important decision, or offer feedback perceived as unfair. In psychologically unsafe teams, such events go unspoken, creating emotional residue that slowly erodes collaboration. Teams may begin to second-guess one another, avoid confrontation, or revert to self-protective behaviours that undermine transparency.

By contrast, in trust-aware teams, repair is intentional and embedded into the culture. The team develops a shared understanding that conflict and failure are not endpoints, but invitations for dialogue. Agile ceremonies, viz. Retrospectives, Sprint Reviews, and Daily Stand-ups, offer structured spaces where misalignments can be named and addressed. More importantly, there is a cultural willingness to have the difficult conversation which involves acknowledging impact, offering accountability, and recommitting to shared values.

Effective trust repair involves three key behaviours:

- **Acknowledgements**: openly recognising that something has gone wrong, without minimising or deflecting. This requires humility and psychological safety.
- **Explanation and Accountability**: providing context for what occurred, while taking responsibility for one's role. This helps depersonalise the breach and restore credibility.
- **Recommitment**: affirming a shared intention to move forward, often with specific actions or boundaries to prevent recurrence.

Leaders and senior team members play a critical modelling role here. When they publicly admit their own missteps and invite feedback, they signal that repair is both acceptable and expected. This not only diffuses power imbalances but normalises imperfection as part of the human (and Agile) process.

Trust repair is rarely a single act. It is a series of small steps, i.e. apologies offered, feedback received with grace, support given after miscommunication, that collectively rebuild relational capital. Over time, these acts create a team culture that is not just high-performing, but high-trusting and self-healing.

8.14 Rituals and Routines that Embed Trust

Trust emerges and is cultivated through consistent, intentional practices that signal reliability, inclusion, and shared commitment. In Agile teams, these trust-building mechanisms often take the form of rituals and routines: repeated interactions that carry symbolic and practical weight. When thoughtfully designed and authentically enacted, such practices embed trust into the very fabric of how a team works.

Agile ceremonies themselves, viz. Daily Stand-ups, Sprint Planning, Retrospectives, and Reviews, serve as scaffolding for relational trust. These are not merely operational checkpoints; they are trust rituals. A Daily Stand-up, for instance, signals that the team values visibility and shared responsibility. It offers a micro-opportunity each day to surface obstacles, request support, and demonstrate follow-through. When consistently honoured, these routines build a sense of mutual reliability.

Retrospectives, in particular, are powerful rituals for psychological safety. Teams that treat Retrospectives as protected spaces for reflection, as opposed to blame, create norms of openness and repair. Over time, the act of collectively looking back and learning from experience becomes a cultural habit, reinforcing the idea that growth is valued over perfection.

Beyond formal ceremonies, team-initiated rituals can also play a critical role. These might include informal "wins of the week" shoutouts, dedicated learning hours, rotating facilitators, or check-in rounds at the start of a meeting. Though seemingly small, such routines build relational equity. They signal that people and not just tasks, matter, and that every team member has a voice and presence that is recognised.

Importantly, rituals help stabilise trust during uncertainty. In times of delivery pressure, organisational change, or internal conflict, the continuity of routine offers predictability. Rituals become anchor points, reminding the team who they are and how they work together. This is especially true when other variables are in flux.

However, rituals must remain authentic and adaptive. When they become performative or disconnected from the team's real needs, they can backfire, breeding cynicism. Trust is built by the meanings these rituals convey. The most effective routines evolve with the team, co-owned and co-adapted over time.

Ultimately, rituals and routines are where values meet behaviour. They transform abstract commitments, such as openness, respect, and courage, into lived, observable practice. In doing so, they create the rhythm of trust that sustains Agile teams through challenge, change, and growth.

8.15 Strategic Implications for Knowledge Sharing

Knowledge sharing in Agile teams is often framed as a behavioural or cultural practice. However, its most enduring effects emerge when it is embedded strategically into the design of teams. When collaboration is treated as an architectural priority rather than an interpersonal bonus, teams become more adaptive, resilient, and generative. They can deliver consistently. In addition, they can learn and evolve, even amid uncertainty and change.

At the heart of this design mindset is the understanding that knowledge is a collective asset. In high-performing Agile teams, expertise is not hoarded for status or control but shared to build capability across roles, domains, and career stages. This orientation requires a shift from dependency on individual contributors to an ecosystem where learning and teaching are mutual responsibilities.

To make this possible, teams must intentionally cultivate structural mechanisms that support knowledge diffusion. These include:

- **Cross-skilling:** encouraging team members to develop fluency in areas adjacent to their core expertise fosters both agility and empathy. Developers who understand testing, testers who understand UX, or product owners who grasp basic technical trade-offs contribute to more coherent decisions and reduce bottlenecks. Cross-skilling is important because it facilitates building *interdependence with range.*
- **Mentorship roles:** both formal and informal mentorship pathways ensure that institutional knowledge is transmitted within the team. Beyond onboarding, ongoing peer mentorship supports faster learning curves, stronger relational ties, and a culture where asking questions is seen as a strength, not a weakness.
- **Rotating responsibilities:** sharing roles such as Sprint facilitator, Retrospective lead, or code reviewer distributes authority and demystifies processes. It also exposes team members to the full system of delivery, which strengthens systems thinking and increases ownership. Role rotation is particularly valuable for surfacing latent leadership potential and reducing dependency on single individuals.

These design choices have tangible implications for onboarding, retention, and long-term capability. When newcomers join a team where knowledge is shared freely and systems are transparent, they integrate more quickly. Retention improves when individuals feel they are growing and contributing, not simply executing. Most importantly, capability does not vanish with attrition. In systems designed for knowledge continuity, teams can absorb turnover without eroding performance.

From a leadership perspective, designing for knowledge sharing is an investment in team sustainability. It shifts the focus from individual brilliance to collective competence, i.e. from heroic effort to habitual learning. It also supports equity: when knowledge is openly shared, access to contribution and advancement is no longer reserved for those with insider status or technical gatekeeping power.

Strategically embedded knowledge sharing is architected not accidental. It is reflected in hiring practices, team norms, career progression frameworks, and even tooling decisions. Agile teams that recognise this embed learning into their operating system, as well as their rituals.

Ultimately, resilient teams don't just protect knowledge. They propagate it, deliberately, inclusively, and continuously. In doing so, they safeguard their present capability, and they invest in their future potential.

8.16 Sharing Knowledge, Growing Together

At the heart of Agile lies a deceptively simple principle: *people over process*. It is a reminder that no matter how sophisticated the tools, no matter how refined the workflows, the real engine of progress is human connection. And at the centre of that connection is knowledge as a living, relational force.

When teams share knowledge openly and safely, they amplify capability. They create environments where insight is not guarded, but freely shared; where questions are not feared but welcomed; and where learning is not confined to Retrospectives but woven into every interaction. In these teams, collaboration is both efficient and enriching. People leave meetings smarter, not smaller. They grow not just as specialists, but as contributors to something larger than themselves.

This kind of open, trust-based collaboration is a defining strength of Agile. However, it is fragile. It requires psychological safety to thrive: the shared belief that one can speak up, make mistakes, challenge assumptions, or admit uncertainty without fear of punishment or exclusion. Without this safety, knowledge flow becomes blocked by ego, silence, or performance anxiety. And when knowledge is trapped, so too is potential.

But when safety is present i.e. when leaders model vulnerability, when feedback is treated as a gift, and when rituals create space for reflection, something powerful happens. Teams begin to build not only software, but a shared understanding. They move from coordination to co-creation, from individual expertise to collective intelligence.

This is the deeper promise of Agile: not just faster features but learning teams. Teams that adapt, reflect, and regenerate. Teams that solve hard problems through generosity of knowledge, of attention, and of trust. These are the teams that grow stronger under pressure, because their strength is distributed, not concentrated.

As Agile practitioners, educators, and leaders, the task, in addition to improving processes is to nurture the conditions in which this kind of collaboration becomes possible. To design teams not just for throughput, but for thoughtfulness. To value not just *what* is delivered, but *how* it is discovered and *who* gets to participate in that discovery.

When teams share knowledge generously, they deliver more than working software. They build capability. They build connection. They build strong and resilient Agile teams.

8.17 Concluding Remarks

This chapter has explored the deep interplay between collaboration, trust, and knowledge sharing in Agile teams as lived practices embedded in culture, structure, and mindset. Moving from communication to collaboration requires a shift in orientation. It is the recognition that effective Agile teams do not merely exchange information; they co-create meaning, co-own delivery, and co-evolve capability.

At the centre of this transformation lies psychological safety: the bedrock upon which all meaningful collaboration rests. Without it, knowledge hoards, dissent silences, and rituals devolve into performance. With it, teams begin to share courageously, reflect purposefully, and learn in the open. Safety is what enables curiosity to displace defensiveness, and feedback to become a gift rather than a threat.

Yet safety alone is insufficient. Collaboration must also be architected into the team's design, through cross-skilling, mentorship, shared rituals, and intentional role rotation. It must be supported by tools that amplify connection, not abstract it; guided by leadership that models humility and transparency; and sustained by cultural practices that turn trust into habit and learning into rhythm.

Importantly, collaboration it is a continuous craft. Teams that thrive revisit and repair their working relationships with the same attention they give to their code. They make space for recalibration, and they treat breakdowns not as failures, but as invitations to grow.

As Agile continues to expand into new domains and complexities, the teams that will endure are those who treat collaboration as a strategic asset. Because in the end, it is not the ceremonies, artefacts, or metrics that define team success, rather it is the quality of connection. And it is in those connections that innovation, resilience, and shared intelligence truly take root.

Agility, at its best, is not about moving faster. It is about learning together, adapting together, and succeeding together. And that begins with people.

References

Cockburn, A., & Highsmith, J. (2002). Agile software development, the people factor. *Computer, 34*(11), 131–133.

Tuckman, B. W. (1965). Developmental sequence in small groups. *Psychological Bulletin, 63*(6), 384.

Chapter 9
Feedback, Continuous Improvement, and Knowledge Retention

Abstract In complex, adaptive work environments, an Agile team's ability to learn and evolve determines its effectiveness. This chapter introduces a framework built upon three intrinsically linked practices that form self-reinforcing learning loops: ongoing feedback, structured continuous improvement, and intentional knowledge retention. These practices are presented as operational tools, but also as foundational mechanisms for cultivating essential team trust. Feedback provides the raw material for learning by surfacing problems and aligning expectations. Continuous improvement operationalises this feedback into concrete actions and adapted processes. Knowledge retention ensures that the lessons learned are preserved and cumulative, rather than transient. Crucially, these loops build trust by fostering psychological safety. When team members engage transparently and non-defensively in these activities, they demonstrate accountability and mutual respect, reducing uncertainty about intentions and competence. Timely, constructive feedback transforms potential conflict into opportunities for collective growth. This approach shifts feedback from a transactional event to a relational, collaborative practice that strengthens resilience, adaptability, and sustained high performance, moving teams beyond superficial process adoption to a genuine culture of collaboration.

9.1 Introduction

In complex, adaptive work environments, the ability of teams to learn and evolve is a decisive factor in their effectiveness. Agile teams succeed through continuous cycles of feedback, improvement, and knowledge retention that enable them to adapt to change, solve emerging problems, and maintain collective focus on delivering value.

This chapter examines three interlinked practices at the heart of effective team functioning:

- **Feedback**: the ongoing exchange of observations, perspectives, and evaluations that surfaces problems early and aligns expectations.
- **Continuous Improvement**: the deliberate, structured effort to reflect on performance, identify opportunities, and experiment with better ways of working.

T. O'Connell, *Trust in Agile Teams*,
SpringerBriefs in Computer Science, https://doi.org/10.1007/978-3-032-21963-3_9

- **Knowledge Retention**: the capture, sharing, and preservation of both explicit and tacit knowledge so that learning is not lost but builds cumulatively over time.

Though these practices are often discussed separately, they are inextricably connected. Feedback provides the raw material for learning by revealing gaps, tensions, or unexpected successes. Continuous improvement uses that feedback to adapt processes, behaviours, and tools in pursuit of better outcomes. Knowledge retention ensures that what is learned is not transient or lost when individuals move on but becomes part of the team's collective capability.

The central focus of this chapter is that feedback, continuous improvement, and knowledge retention work as learning loops that reinforce and deepen trust over time. Trust emerges, grows, and is sustained through repeated experiences in which team members demonstrate transparency, accountability, and shared commitment to learning. Trust is not a static condition.

When teams consistently give and receive feedback well, they create an environment of psychological safety, where it is acceptable to discuss failures, challenge assumptions, and surface dissenting views. When they engage in structured reflection and continuous improvement, they demonstrate their willingness to act on that feedback, signalling respect for one another's insights and a shared investment in collective success. And when they retain and share knowledge intentionally, they reduce the risk of avoidable mistakes, preserve hard-won learning, and make it easier for new members to integrate and contribute.

These intertwined practices are, in effect, trust-building loops. They reduce uncertainty about others' intentions and competence, signal mutual respect, and create a reliable, predictable environment in which vulnerability is safe. In doing so, they strengthen the team's resilience and adaptability over time.

In the sections that follow, this chapter will:

- Examine feedback as a core mechanism for surfacing truth and aligning expectations.
- Explore continuous improvement practices that operationalise learning at the team level.
- Analyse strategies for effective knowledge retention and sharing, particularly in Agile and distributed contexts.
- Connect these practices back to the central challenge of building and maintaining trust in collaborative work.

By understanding these practices as interconnected learning loops, teams and organisations can move beyond superficial process adoption to cultivate cultures of genuine collaboration, adaptability, and sustained high performance.

9.2 Feedback as a Trust-Building Practice

Feedback is often seen narrowly as a transaction, i.e. a delivery of information from one person to another about performance. But in effective teams, feedback is fundamentally relational. It is a practice that both depends on and builds trust. Through feedback, team members reveal their expectations, acknowledge interdependence, and demonstrate commitment to shared goals.

As Cockburn and Highsmith (2002) suggest in the context of Agile development, collaboration is about actively working together to deliver outcomes. Feedback, in this sense, is not merely the exchange of information but a collaborative act of joint problem-solving and mutual adjustment. It is a signal of respect, i.e. taking the time to share observations, offer constructive critique, or ask for clarification reflects belief in the other's capacity to improve and a willingness to invest in the relationship.

Timely, respectful, and constructive feedback reinforces trust in multiple ways by:

- **Showing care**: by offering feedback, team members show they care about one another's success and the quality of the team's output.
- **Demonstrating commitment**: this signals investment in shared goals and the team's long-term effectiveness.
- **Reducing uncertainty**: feedback clarifies expectations and surfaces misunderstandings before they can erode confidence or derail work.
- **Modelling vulnerability**: giving and receiving feedback requires openness, which invites reciprocal transparency and deepens trust.

As Tabaka (2006) argues, Agile teams declare a "collaborative imperative" when they commit to participatory decision-making and continuous learning. Feedback is one of the most direct expressions of that commitment. In Scrum, for example, ceremonies such as the Sprint Review and Sprint Retrospective explicitly institutionalise feedback loops to ensure that the team inspects and adapts its work and processes together.

Yet despite its potential to build trust, feedback is often difficult in practice. Several barriers to effective feedback are common and include:

- **Fear of conflict**: team members may worry that feedback will be taken personally, damage relationships, or provoke defensive reactions.
- **Hierarchy and power dynamics**: in hierarchical cultures or organisations, subordinates may be reluctant to speak candidly to superiors, while managers may fear demotivating staff.
- **Cultural differences**: expectations about directness, politeness, and deference vary significantly across cultures, leading to misunderstandings or avoidance.
- **Low psychological safety**: if people fear blame or punishment for mistakes, they will withhold honest feedback, and opportunities for learning will be lost.

To overcome these barriers, teams can focus on enablers of effective feedback, which can include:

- **Norms of candour and empathy**: establishing explicit team norms that encourage honest but respectful feedback helps normalise the practice. Framing feedback as an expression of care and shared responsibility reduces defensiveness.
- **Psychological safety**: leaders and team members alike can model vulnerability by soliciting feedback themselves, acknowledging their own fallibility, and responding non-defensively.
- **Framing feedback as collective improvement**: rather than focusing on individual blame, feedback can be positioned as a tool for the team's collective learning and adaptation. This aligns with the Agile principle of continuous improvement and reinforces the idea that everyone benefits from shared reflection.

For trust to flourish it is vital that understanding, mutual respect, and trust must develop during the collaborative process. Feedback is one of the most direct ways teams can nurture that respect and understanding. By viewing feedback not as a criticism but as a joint effort to improve, teams can transform it from a source of anxiety into a core trust-building practice.

In the next section, how feedback is operationalised through turning insights into concrete, collective change will be explored.

9.3 Models and Tools for Feedback

While the value of feedback as a trust-building, learning-enabling practice is clear, many teams struggle with *how* to deliver it well. Without structure, feedback conversations can become vague, personal, or confrontational, which can undermine the very trust that the feedback is meant to build. Structured feedback models provide scaffolding that helps teams offer clear, actionable, and respectful feedback while reinforcing norms of openness and psychological safety.

Below are some widely used models and tools that teams can adapt to their needs:

9.3.1 SBI (Situation–Behaviour–Impact) Model

The SBI framework offers a simple, disciplined approach to feedback by anchoring observations in specific contexts. It helps avoid personal attacks or vague judgements by structuring feedback in three steps:

- **Situation**: describe the context clearly and precisely. *"During yesterday's client meeting..."*
- **Behaviour**: focus on observable, specific actions. *"...you interrupted the client several times..."*
- **Impact**: explain the effect of the behaviour. *"...which made it hard for them to share their concerns."*

By separating observation from interpretation, the SBI model reduces defensiveness and supports mutual understanding. It is especially useful in teams with diverse backgrounds or roles, where assumptions can easily lead to misunderstandings.

9.3.2 Radical Candor

Kim Scott's *Radical Candor* model has gained popularity for emphasising that the most effective feedback balances care personally with challenge directly (Scott, 2019). Feedback that is too cautious can become unhelpfully vague ("ruinous empathy"), while feedback that is brutally honest but uncaring can be demotivating ("obnoxious aggression").

Radical Candor invites team members to:

- **Care Personally**: build relationships of genuine respect and concern.
- **Challenge Directly**: be willing to speak hard truths clearly and kindly.

In Agile contexts, where rapid learning and adaptation are crucial, this model aligns well with cultural values of openness and mutual support.

9.3.3 Start–Stop–Continue

This simple yet powerful retrospective tool invites team members to share:

- **Start**: new practices or behaviours to adopt.
- **Stop**: unhelpful behaviours or practices to end.
- **Continue**: valuable practices worth sustaining.

Its structured, balanced format lowers the stakes of feedback by framing it as a shared exercise in collective improvement. It also helps teams avoid blame by focusing on specific actions rather than personal traits.

9.3.4 Retrospectives (Agile Context)

Retrospectives are a core Agile practice explicitly designed to institutionalise feedback and continuous improvement. At the end of each iteration or sprint, the team reflects on:

- ***What went well?***
- ***What didn't go well?***
- ***What will we do differently next time?***

Retrospectives provide a regular, predictable forum for feedback, helping to normalise honest discussion and problem-solving. By making reflection part of the team's rhythm, they reinforce psychological safety and signal that learning from experience is valued.

9.3.5 Structured Peer Feedback (360-Degree, Paired Reviews)

For more formalised settings, tools like 360-degree feedback (where feedback is collected from peers, managers, and direct reports) or paired reviews (structured one-on-one feedback conversations) can be used to broaden perspectives and reduce bias.

Such methods encourage self-awareness by exposing individuals to varied viewpoints, while also making feedback a reciprocal, shared practice. However, these tools require high levels of trust and clear norms to avoid defensiveness or misuse.

9.3.6 Aligning Feedback Tools to Team Culture

No feedback model is one-size-fits-all. Effective feedback practices must be tailored to a team's culture, context, and maturity:

- **Psychological safety** is a prerequisite: Without it, even the best tools will fail.
- **Cultural norms** around hierarchy and communication style must be considered to avoid unintended offence or silence.
- **Team goals and rhythm** matter. Tools should fit the cadence of work and support shared outcomes.

Selecting the right feedback tools involves understanding the team's needs and co-creating practices that feel safe, relevant, and useful. In the end, models and tools are just enablers. The true goal is to embed feedback as a shared norm and ongoing habit that strengthens trust, learning, and performance.

9.4 Continuous Improvement as a Cultural Practice

Continuous improvement is a mindset and cultural practice that underpins sustained team effectiveness. Rooted in principles such as *Kaizen* (a Japanese term meaning "change for the better" or continuous, incremental improvement), this approach emphasises frequent, deliberate reflection and adaptation.

In Agile software development, this principle is embodied in practices like Retrospectives, where teams pause at regular intervals to assess what went well, what fell short, and how they might improve. The Agile Manifesto itself enshrines this commitment: *"At regular intervals, the team reflects on how to become more effective, then tunes and adjusts its behaviour accordingly"* (Beck et al., 2001).

9.4.1 Continuous Improvement and Trust

At its heart, continuous improvement depends on trust. Teams cannot reflect honestly on their shortcomings without a sense of psychological safety. Two essential dimensions illustrate this link:

- **Vulnerability**: admitting what didn't work, acknowledging mistakes, or proposing changes to established practices demands personal and collective vulnerability. Without trust, team members will avoid raising issues for fear of blame, conflict, or retribution.
- **Shared Commitment**: improvement is about acting on insights. Trust ensures that commitments made during Retrospectives or Sprint reviews are meaningful, that everyone feels accountable to the group, and that improvements will be pursued in good faith.

In this way, continuous improvement practices create learning loops that, in addition to addressing technical or process issues, also reinforce trust over time. Teams see that their honesty leads to real change, making them more willing to share candid feedback in the future.

9.4.2 Barriers to Continuous Improvement

Despite its benefits, continuous improvement faces well-known obstacles:

- **Blame Cultures**: in environments where mistakes are punished or scapegoated, people naturally hide problems. Blame cultures stifle the learning on which continuous improvement depends.
- **Lip Service Without Follow-Through**: teams may go through the motions of Retrospectives or lessons-learned sessions without enacting change. When reflection becomes performative rather than genuine, trust is eroded, and team members learn that their input doesn't matter.
- **Fear of Conflict**: discussing what didn't work can surface tensions or disagreements. Without norms for respectful dialogue, teams may avoid important topics or let resentments simmer.

9.4.3 Enablers of Continuous Improvement

Effective continuous improvement cultures require deliberate, supportive conditions. Key enablers include:

- **Leadership Modelling**: Leaders should play a crucial role in signalling that it is safe to acknowledge problems. When leaders admit their own mistakes, seek feedback, and act on suggestions, they set the tone for open, honest reflection.
- **Psychological Safety to Critique Systems, Not People**: teams must cultivate the norm that improvement discussions target processes, not personal blame. Framing issues as systemic enables constructive problem-solving and reduces defensiveness.
- **Ritualised Practices**: create regular, structured opportunities for reflection, such as Retrospectives, learning reviews, or improvement experiments. These can help normalise candid dialogue. Rituals create a predictable space where critique is expected and valued.
- **Visible Follow-Through**: acting on improvement insights is essential. Even small changes that address raised issues show the team that their reflections matter and build credibility for the process.

Ultimately, continuous improvement is a social contract within the team. Team members agree to be honest about what isn't working, to listen to one another, and to commit to working together to make things better. When practised well, it becomes a virtuous cycle, deepening trust while enabling the team to adapt, innovate, and sustain high performance over time.

9.5 Learning Loops and Trust Feedback Cycles

Continuous improvement and feedback form learning loops that drive team development over time. At their core, these loops represent the way teams convert experience into knowledge and adapt their practices in response.

A well-known conceptual framework for understanding these learning loops comes from Argyris and Schön (Clark, 2021), who distinguish between single-loop and double-loop learning:

- **Single-Loop Learning** involves detecting and correcting errors within existing frameworks, policies, or assumptions. It's akin to adjusting the thermostat when the room is too hot or cold by making incremental changes without questioning the underlying goals or strategies.
- **Double-Loop Learning** goes deeper. It involves reflecting on and, if necessary, changing the underlying assumptions, values, or norms that guide behaviour. Using the thermostat analogy, double-loop learning asks: *Why is the thermostat set this way? Do we need a new heating system? Is our comfort goal appropriate?*

In a team context, single-loop learning might mean tweaking how a stand-up meeting is run to make it more efficient. Double-loop learning would involve questioning whether the team's approach to communication or decision-making genuinely supports its goals, perhaps challenging entrenched roles or assumptions.

9.5.1 Why Double-Loop Learning Requires Deeper Trust

Single-loop learning can be relatively easy to implement. This is because it is about improving within safe boundaries. However, double-loop learning is inherently riskier. It asks team members to question the *why* behind what they do, which can threaten established power dynamics, expose hidden disagreements, or challenge personal or group identities.

For double-loop learning to succeed, teams must cultivate:

- **Psychological Safety**: members need to know they can voice doubts or challenge assumptions without fear of ridicule, punishment, or exclusion.
- **Mutual Respect**: deep inquiry requires listening to and valuing diverse perspectives, even when they are uncomfortable or disruptive.
- **Commitment to Shared Goals**: without a strong sense of collective purpose, critical reflection can degenerate into unproductive conflict or blame.

Trust, therefore, is the foundation for learning.

9.5.2 The "Trust Spiral"

This dynamic can be visualised as a trust spiral, where each cycle of feedback and learning strengthens the team's trust and capacity to adapt. The Trust Spiral involves:

- **Open Sharing**: team members speak candidly about successes, failures, and uncertainties.
- **Collective Learning**: the group reflects on this feedback to identify both surface-level fixes and deeper shifts in thinking.
- **Improved Outcomes**: changes lead to better processes, solutions, or relationships.
- **Increased Trust**: seeing that openness leads to real improvement reinforces members' willingness to share candidly in the future.

Each successful turn of the spiral strengthens the team's resilience and adaptability, enabling them to handle greater complexity and uncertainty together.

9.5.3 Learning Loops in Agile (Inspect and Adapt)

Agile methodologies embed learning loops at their core through practices like Sprint Retrospectives and Inspect-and-Adapt cycles:

- Single-loop learning in a retrospective might involve adjusting how tasks are assigned or clarifying Sprint goals.
- Double-loop learning might involve rethinking the team's definition of "Done," challenging assumptions about stakeholder communication, or reconsidering the balance between speed and quality.

By making these cycles routine and expected, Agile frameworks create ritualised spaces for reflection, reducing the interpersonal risk of candour. Over time, these loops become powerful drivers of both continuous improvement and deepening trust.

9.6 Knowledge Retention and Organisational Memory

As teams strive for continuous improvement and adaptability, they must also safeguard the knowledge they create along the way. Knowledge retention refers to the practices that ensure valuable learning, which can be both explicit (documented, codified) and tacit (personal, experiential). Learning is captured and made accessible for current and future team members.

Effective knowledge retention is deeply tied to trust within teams and organisations.

9.6.1 Capturing Tacit and Explicit Knowledge

- Explicit knowledge includes formal artefacts like design documents, user stories, architectural decision records (ADRs), and process guides. This knowledge can be codified, stored, and widely shared.
- Tacit knowledge is embedded in individual experience, i.e. insights, intuitions, and contextual understanding that are harder to write down but essential for problem-solving and innovation. Sharing tacit knowledge often requires close interpersonal interaction, like pairing, mentoring, or storytelling.

Both forms are critical. Without explicit knowledge, teams risk reinvention and inconsistency. Without tacit knowledge transfer, documentation becomes hollow, i.e. divorced from the practical wisdom that gives it life.

9.6.2 Link to Trust: Vulnerability and Collective Stewardship

Knowledge sharing is inherently vulnerable. Team members may be anxious about:

- **Job Security Fears:** individuals may fear that documenting or sharing their expertise makes them replaceable.
- **Reputation Concerns**: sharing failures or lessons learned openly can feel risky, especially in blame-oriented cultures.

Trust is the lubricant that makes knowledge sharing possible. When team members believe their contributions will be valued rather than exploited, they are more willing to make their know-how visible.

Conversely, collective stewardship, which describes the norm that "*we are all responsible for our shared knowledge,*" reinforces trust by signalling a commitment to the team's continuity and success beyond any individual.

9.6.3 Challenges to Knowledge Retention

Several common barriers can undermine effective organisational memory. These include:

- **Turnover:** high attrition can result in critical expertise walking out the door, especially if it was never documented or shared.
- **Siloed Expertise:** when knowledge is hoarded within specialised roles or sub-teams, it becomes fragile and consequently harder to access or adapt when needs change.
- **Resistance to Documentation:** teams may see documentation as overhead, irrelevant, or risky, especially if past efforts were misused for blame or control.

These challenges are cultural, reflecting underlying assumptions about ownership, value, and safety.

9.6.4 Enablers of Knowledge Retention

To address these barriers, teams can adopt practices that both capture knowledge and reinforce trust:

- **Pairing and Mentoring**: collaborative work practices that support real-time transfer of tacit knowledge. Pair programming or mentorship relationships make sharing safe, routine, and relational.
- **Knowledge Bases and Wikis**: living repositories that democratise access to explicit knowledge, provided they are maintained and integrated into daily work.

- **Communities of Practice**: voluntary groups that cross team boundaries to share lessons, discuss challenges, and develop shared standards. These communities strengthen social ties and normalise open knowledge exchange.
- **Documentation Rituals**: structured practices such as Architectural Decision Records (ADRs), Postmortems, and Retrospectives help teams systematically reflect, record, and disseminate learning. When these rituals focus on systemic improvement rather than individual blame, they become trust-building exercises.

Ultimately, knowledge retention is about enabling collective intelligence. It depends on a team culture that values openness, mutual learning, and continuity. These foundations can only be built on trust.

9.7 Strategies for Embedding Learning

For teams to thrive over time, learning cannot be left to chance or treated as an afterthought. Instead, it must be intentionally embedded into the fabric of everyday work. This section outlines practical strategies for making learning visible, routine, and valued, so that knowledge is retained, trust is reinforced, and continuous improvement becomes second nature.

9.7.1 Intentional Onboarding Processes

Bringing new team members up to speed is a critical learning moment:

- Effective onboarding goes beyond administrative tasks. It intentionally transfers both explicit knowledge (documentation, tooling, processes) and tacit knowledge (team norms, shared histories, key trade-offs).
- Pairing new hires with experienced team members, conducting welcome retrospectives, or sharing decision logs can reduce ramp-up time and reinforce a culture of openness and mentorship.

A well-designed onboarding process signals that learning is a priority and builds trust by demonstrating the team's commitment to setting each person up for success.

9.7.2 Documenting Decisions

Decisions often carry rich contextual knowledge. Making them explicit helps teams remember not just *what* they chose but *why*:

- **Decision Logs**: simple, consistent records of key design or process choices, with rationales and alternatives considered.

- **Architectural Decision Records (ADRs)**: structured documents capturing significant architectural choices, their context, consequences, and status over time.

These artefacts support learning by avoiding the "*why did we do that?*" trap and reducing repeated debate over settled questions. They also help new team members quickly understand past reasoning, promoting continuity.

9.7.3 Facilitating Reflective Practices

Reflection is the engine of team learning. Structured reflection practices turn experience into improvement:

- **After-Action Reviews**: short, focused sessions after significant events (deployments, incidents, experiments) to identify what went well, what didn't, and what to change.
- **Learning Reviews**: broader retrospectives that look at patterns across projects or time periods to extract systemic insights.

These practices require psychological safety: the trust that team members can speak honestly about missteps without fear of blame. When done well, they make continuous improvement real rather than rhetorical.

9.7.4 Using Tooling to Support Retention

Technology can amplify knowledge sharing if used deliberately:

- **Wikis and Knowledge Bases**: living repositories for team practices, decisions, and documentation that are easy to search and maintain.
- **Knowledge Graphs**: tools that map relationships among concepts, decisions, and stakeholders, helping teams navigate complex domains.

The key is not the tool itself but making it integral to daily work so that knowledge is not only captured but also used and updated.

9.7.5 Cultural Enablers

Beyond tools and processes, sustained learning depends on culture:

- **Valuing Learning Time**: protecting time for Retrospectives, documentation, mentoring, and training. It is important to prioritise these even when delivery pressures mount.

- **Recognising Contributions to Shared Knowledge**: celebrating those who write clear documentation, teach others, or improve team practices. This reinforces that learning is part of everyone's job, not an extra burden.

A culture that values learning sees it not as cost, but as investment. It is an investment that pays off with greater trust, resilience, and adaptability.

By embedding these strategies into their everyday routines, teams can make learning visible, habitual, and shared. This creates the foundation for continuous improvement, knowledge retention, and the kind of deep trust that enables sustained, effective collaboration.

9.8 Leadership's Role in Enabling Learning and Trust

Even with the right tools and processes, a team's capacity to learn, improve, and retain knowledge hinges on leadership. Leaders set the tone for how safe it feels to share ideas, admit mistakes, and challenge assumptions. Their actions can either reinforce trust and learning or undermine them. Ways in which leaders can reinforce trust include:

9.8.1 Role Modelling Vulnerability

Trust starts at the top. When leaders are willing to:

- Admit they don't have all the answers
- Share their own mistakes and learning moments
- Acknowledgements uncertainty in complex situations

They show that vulnerability is not weakness but a foundation for collective problem-solving. This openness encourages team members to take similar risks, such as offering dissenting views or surfacing problems early. Over time, it normalises the idea that everyone is learning and that learning together is valued.

9.8.2 Creating Space for Reflection

Reflection doesn't happen by accident, especially in high-pressure environments:

- Leaders who prioritise and protect time for Retrospectives, after-action reviews, and learning sessions signal that these practices are essential, not optional.
- They ensure these sessions are meaningful by participating fully, asking thoughtful questions, and following through on insights.

By creating space for reflection, leaders help teams turn experience into actionable learning, reinforcing the feedback loops that sustain improvement and trust.

9.8.3 Rewarding Learning Over Blaming

Blame cultures shut down learning. Team members who fear reprisal for mistakes hide problems rather than fix them. Effective leaders:

- Shift the focus from "*Who is at fault*?" to "*What can we learn*?"
- Publicly recognise those who surface issues early or who share lessons from failures.
- Reward experimentation, even when outcomes are uncertain, as long as learning is extracted.

These reframing builds trust by demonstrating that the team is committed to collective growth over individual blame.

9.8.4 Allocating Time and Resources for Improvement

Continuous improvement can't flourish on goodwill alone. It requires investment:

- Allocating time in sprints for refactoring, documentation, or process improvements.
- Supporting training, mentoring, and cross-functional learning.
- Ensuring access to tools and platforms that enable knowledge sharing.

When leaders invest in improvement they show they value long-term capability over short-term output. This commitment reinforces trust by aligning words with actions.

9.8.5 Building a Shared Vision of a Learning Culture

Finally, leaders play a critical role in articulating and reinforcing a shared vision of what it means to be a learning organisation. This includes:

- Setting clear expectations that learning is everyone's responsibility.
- Framing challenges and failures as opportunities to grow, not threats to avoid.
- Celebrating collective progress, not just individual achievement.

By communicating a compelling vision of continuous learning and improvement and consistently acting in alignment with it, leaders help embed these values into the team's identity. This shared vision fosters cohesion, purpose, and trust, making learning not an afterthought but a defining feature of how the team works.

Ultimately, leadership is about creating the conditions in which teams can safely and effectively learn, share knowledge, and improve together. By modelling vulnerability, making time for reflection, rewarding learning over blame, investing in improvement, and building a shared vision of a learning culture, leaders lay the foundation for sustained trust and high performance.

9.9 The Interplay of Feedback, Improvement, and Retention

Feedback, continuous improvement, and knowledge retention are often discussed as separate practices, but in reality, they form an integrated system, a set of learning loops that drive team effectiveness and resilience. Treating them in isolation risks fragmenting efforts that only work when they reinforce each other.

9.9.1 *Feedback Informs Improvement*

Effective feedback acts as a catalyst for improvement within teams. When team members share candid and constructive observations about what is working and what is not, they surface problems early before they escalate, highlight areas of strength that can be further developed, and encourage open dialogue about challenges. Through this process, teams are better able to adapt their processes, refine their practices, and address potential blind spots. In the absence of feedback, teams risk stagnation, the repetition of mistakes, and missed opportunities to build on their successes.

9.9.2 *Improvement Produces New Learning*

Continuous improvement represents the structured response to feedback, transforming observations into purposeful action. Through retrospectives, experimentation, and iterative process adjustments, teams test new approaches and learn what works, refine workflows and clarify expectations, and adapt to changing contexts, requirements, or team composition. Each cycle of improvement generates new learning that strengthens the team's capability, adaptability, and collective confidence.

9.9.3 Retention Ensures Learning is not Lost

However, improvement alone is insufficient if the learning it generates is not retained. Knowledge retention practices capture insights from retrospectives, postmortems, and experiments. They document decisions, trade-offs, and their underlying rationale for future reference. Furthermore, they enable the sharing of expertise through pairing, mentoring, and communities of practice. By preserving and transferring learning, retention ensures that knowledge benefits not only the current team but also safeguards future teams against the risks associated with turnover, scaling challenges, and the loss of institutional memory.

9.9.4 Learning as a Team Process

Critically, these practices are social at their core and depend on strong interpersonal foundations. They rely on robust social bonds in which members trust one another enough to give and receive honest feedback. Having shared norms that prioritise candour over politeness and collective goals over individual ego lowers the cost of vulnerability required to admit mistakes, propose changes, and teach others. Teams that treat feedback, improvement, and knowledge retention as collective responsibilities cultivate deeper cohesion and resilience.

9.9.5 Reinforcing Trust Through Learning Loops

These learning loops extend beyond improvements in delivery or quality; they actively contribute to the development of trust within teams. By acting on feedback and sustaining improvements, teams demonstrate reliability and show that they can be counted on to learn and adapt. Honest, respectful feedback and the sharing of knowledge signal care and a genuine commitment to one another's success, while working collaboratively to improve and retain learning reflects a shared purpose and alignment around goals and values. Over time, these reinforcing dynamics create a "trust flywheel," in which sharing, improvement, and retention strengthen trust, and growing trust in turn makes future learning easier and more effective.

By seeing feedback, improvement, and knowledge retention as a single, integrated system, teams can avoid siloed efforts and cultivate the kind of high-trust, high-learning environment that is essential for sustained success.

Table 9.1 A summary of barriers and enablers for effective team functioning practices

Practice	Common barriers	Enablers
Feedback	– Fear of conflict – Hierarchical power dynamics – Cultural differences – Low psychological safety	– Norms of candour and empathy – Framing feedback as collective improvement – Timely, respectful delivery – Shared feedback models (e.g. SBI, etc.)
Continuous improvement	– Blame cultures – Lip service but no follow through – Fear of admitting mistakes	– Leadership modelling vulnerability – Psychological safety – Ritualised practices (e.g. Retrospectives etc.) - Shared commitment to experimentation
Knowledge retention	– High turnover – Siloed expertise – Resistance to documentation – Perceived time cost	– Pairing and mentoring – Knowledge bases, wikis – Communities of practice – Documenting decisions (e.g. ADRs etc.) – Valuing knowledge sharing opportunities

9.10 Barriers and Enablers: A Summary Table

To make these ideas actionable, the Table 9.1 summarises common barriers and enabling practices across feedback, continuous improvement, and knowledge retention. This serves as a practical reference for teams seeking to strengthen their learning culture and build trust.

9.11 Concluding Remarks

In complex, adaptive work environments, the ability of teams to learn and evolve is a decisive factor in sustained effectiveness. This chapter has explored how feedback, continuous improvement, and knowledge retention function as interlinked learning loops that both depend on and reinforce trust.

Teams that invest in these loops build trust incrementally, through repeated, tangible demonstrations of care, competence, and shared commitment. Feedback surfaces truth early and aligns expectations, showing that team members respect each other enough to speak honestly. Continuous improvement turns that feedback into meaningful change, signalling that the team values learning over blame and is willing to act together on its insights. Knowledge retention ensures that this hard-won learning is not lost to turnover or forgotten over time but instead becomes part of the team's collective capability.

Together, these practices form a virtuous cycle:

- Feedback reveals problems and opportunities.
- Improvement addresses them, building credibility and showing responsiveness.
- Retention preserves and shares learning, enabling new members to integrate quickly and existing members to deepen their understanding.

Each turn of this cycle strengthens trust, making future feedback easier, learning richer, and improvement more robust.

However, cultivating these loops requires deliberate, ongoing cultural work. Teams must create and maintain psychological safety i.e. a space where vulnerability is met with respect rather than blame. Leaders must model openness, prioritise reflection, and invest in learning as an integral part of work, not an optional add-on. Teams must establish and maintain shared norms that value candour, empathy, and collective stewardship of knowledge.

Ultimately, these practices are social at their core. They rely on strong relationships, mutual understanding, and a sense of shared purpose. By embedding learning loops into the daily rhythm of work, teams move toward a culture of continuous, collaborative improvement.

For Agile teams, these trust-building loops are essential. Agile methods promise responsiveness, adaptability, and customer focus. However, these outcomes depend on the team's capacity to learn together. Without feedback, improvement stalls. Without trust, feedback dries up. Without retention, teams repeat old mistakes.

By recognising and intentionally nurturing these connections, teams can create a resilient foundation for sustained high performance built on deep, mutual trust.

References

Beck, K., Beedle, M., Van Bennekum, A., Cockburn, A., Cunningham, W., Fowler, M., ... & Thomas, D. (2001). Manifesto for agile software development.

Clark, K. M. (2021). Double-loop learning and productive reasoning: Chris Argyris's contributions to a framework for lifelong learning and inquiry. *Midwest Social Sciences Journal, 24*(1), 6.

Cockburn, A., & Highsmith, J. (2002). Agile software development, the people factor. *Computer, 34*(11), 131–133.

Scott, K. (2019). *Radical Candor: Fully revised & updated edition: Be a kick-ass boss without losing your humanity.* Martin's Press.

Tabaka, J. (2006). *Collaboration explained: facilitation skills for software project leaders.* Pearson Education.

Chapter 10
Scaling Trust in Large Agile Organisations

Abstract Agile methodologies emerged from small, co-located teams where trust developed organically through proximity, shared context, and frequent interpersonal interaction. As Agile has matured and been adopted at scale, often across distributed, multi-team, and global organisational environments, these implicit trust dynamics have been fundamentally disrupted. What once emerged naturally must now be deliberately designed. This chapter argues that trust represents a critical architectural, cultural, and leadership challenge. When trust is neglected, Agile risks devolving into ritualised compliance, where ceremonies persist but commitment, resilience, and learning erode. Drawing on organisational theory, Agile practice, and empirical insights, the chapter examines why trust becomes more fragile at scale, identifying structural complexity, weakened social ties, communication distortion, competing loyalties, and reduced psychological safety as key contributors. It then explores the foundational conditions required to sustain trust across teams, locations, and leadership layers, integrating structural enablers, communication patterns, and cultural practices. Common anti-patterns that corrode trust are analysed alongside practical strategies for leaders seeking to foster systemic trust through transparency, empathy, and intentional design. Ultimately, the chapter positions scaling trust as a deeply human endeavour and a prerequisite for sustainable agility. Without trust, Agile cannot thrive; with it, even highly complex systems can move with cohesion, clarity, and purpose.

10.1 Introduction

Agile was developed for small, co-located teams. Typically, these teams would be tight-knit groups whose members could turn their chairs to resolve a blocker, gather around a whiteboard to ideate, or spot a struggling teammate without a word being spoken. In such environments, **trust often emerged organically** through proximity, familiarity, and shared accountability. These interpersonal dynamics were so embedded in early Agile practice that they were seldom named, and rarely if ever became problematic.

T. O'Connell, *Trust in Agile Teams*,
SpringerBriefs in Computer Science, https://doi.org/10.1007/978-3-032-21963-3_10

Yet as Agile has matured, it has scaled, and with scale comes strain (Tyagi et al., 2022). Organisations now deploy Agile frameworks across continents, departments, and functions. What once worked effortlessly in a single team room must now be orchestrated across a network of interdependent teams, layered hierarchies, and cultural fault lines. In this shift, **the implicit becomes explicit,** and trust, which was once assumed, is revealed as the hidden constraint.

This chapter argues that **trust is an architectural and cultural condition** that must be consciously designed, sustained, and led. Trust **does not scale automatically,** and it is important to realise it is not a passive by-product of adopting Agile. Without trust, the outer form of Agile may persist, viz. Daily Standups, story points, Sprints, etc., but the inner essence degrades. Teams become compliant rather than committed. Communication becomes procedural rather than relational. Delivery becomes fragile rather than resilient.

In large-scale Agile environments, trust is tested by structural complexity, distributed collaboration, asynchronous communication, and competing priorities. Left unaddressed, these dynamics foster friction, erode psychological safety, and fragment the very alignment that Agile seeks to achieve.

This chapter explores the multidimensional challenge of scaling trust in complex Agile contexts. It begins by diagnosing **why trust becomes harder to maintain at scale,** before examining the **foundational conditions** which are both structural and cultural. It is these foundations that support trust across teams, locations, and leadership layers. It presents patterns for **communication, coordination, and cultural coherence** that sustain trust in distributed systems, and identifies **anti-patterns and leadership pitfalls** that corrode it. Finally, it offers **practical strategies for leaders** who wish to foster systemic trust through transparency, empathy, and intentional design.

Scaling Agile is a deeply human endeavour. And trust, is the hardest infrastructure of all. Without trust agility cannot thrive. With trust even the most complex systems can move with cohesion, clarity, and purpose.

10.2 Scaling Trust in Complex Agile Contexts

Agile methodologies emerged from environments where small, co-located teams could build strong interpersonal bonds, share context rapidly, and adapt collectively. In such settings, trust is often cultivated organically through frequent face-to-face interactions, visible contributions, and shared accountability. The proximity of team members fosters psychological safety, rapid feedback loops, and alignment around common goals.

However, as Agile practices have been adopted at scale, most often across large software development programs, distributed teams, and complex organisational ecosystems, the dynamics of trust shift dramatically. In scaled Agile contexts, teams may span time zones, organisational boundaries, or cultural divides. Communication becomes mediated by tools rather than conversation. Coordination mechanisms are more formalised. The intimacy of a single team room gives way to the complexity of multiple cross-functional units operating in parallel. In such environments, the assumptions underpinning trust in small teams begin to falter.

The core challenge, then, is this: trust does not scale automatically. Rather than being a passive outcome of Agile adoption trust is a cultural and structural condition that must be deliberately cultivated. Without intentional trust-building mechanisms, such as transparent governance, aligned incentives, shared rituals, and strong inter-team relationships, Agile at scale can become fragile, bureaucratic, or superficially collaborative. Mistrust manifests in defensive behaviours, reduced knowledge sharing, and the erosion of collective responsibility.

This chapter argues that scaling trust requires deliberate design and cultural reinforcement. Agile transformations must embed trust as both a design principle and a lived practice, supported by leadership behaviours, enabling infrastructure, and mechanisms for continuous feedback. Without this foundation, the agility of large-scale programs is compromised by relational fragility.

10.3 Why Trust is Harder at Scale

In a small Agile team, trust often feels effortless. It grows from Daily Stand-ups, Retrospectives and even hallway chats, shared victories, and shared frustrations. People know each other's quirks, strengths, and intentions. They can read body language, offer feedback in the moment, and rally quickly around problems. In small teams, trust is immediate and grounded in strong interpersonal ties.

But as Agile is scaled whether this be across departments, time zones, or entire enterprises, something changes. That organic, easy trust just doesn't stretch to fit the larger system. It frays. And if it isn't actively woven back together, the fabric of collaboration starts to unravel. Some of the issues to consider include:

10.3.1 The Disappearance of Strong Ties

In large programs, people become names in Jira, profile pictures in Slack, or titles on an org chart. The strong personal bonds that underpin trust in small teams give way to weaker, more transactional connections. It can happen that you collaborate with someone for months and never meet them. Without shared context or informal touchpoints, assumptions fill the gaps, and these are not always charitable.

10.3.2 Complexity is the Enemy of Clarity

With scale comes complexity: more teams, more dependencies, more moving parts. Coordinating work starts to feel like conducting an orchestra with a dozen conductors and no shared score. When timelines slip or deliverables miss the mark, it's easy for trust to erode because coordination becomes so inherently difficult.

10.3.3 Silos Are Comfortable and Dangerous

As teams grow, they naturally cluster into sub-groups. Sometimes this is by design, and sometimes it occurs by default. These silos often develop their own microcultures and goals. What feels like autonomy inside one team can look like uncooperativeness from another. When teams start to see each other as "*them*" rather than "*us*," trust decays into suspicion.

10.3.4 Messages Lose Fidelity as They Travel

In a single team, miscommunication can be fixed with a quick conversation. But in scaled Agile settings, communication travels across tools, time zones, and organisational layers. Messages get diluted, distorted, or delayed. What was a minor issue in one place becomes a major misunderstanding elsewhere. The resulting noise makes it harder to maintain the clarity and honesty that trust relies on.

10.3.5 The Crowd is Intimidating

Psychological safety. i.e. the freedom to speak candidly without fear, can shrink in large groups. In a small team, people might challenge an idea or admit a mistake. In a program-wide meeting with senior leadership on the call, this is far less likely. The bigger the forum, the greater the pressure to perform or conform, and the less room there is for vulnerability.

10.3.6 Competing Loyalties Create Tension

In matrixed organisations, people are accountable to multiple leaders, goals, and value streams. They may feel torn between their team's sprint goals and a department-level initiative. When priorities clash and no one explains why, suspicion grows. Team members start to wonder: whose interests are you really serving? Trust falters when loyalties are unclear or seemingly misaligned.

In summary, scale magnifies everything, frequently complexity, but scale also poses risks to trust. It introduces distance, noise, and competing agendas that make the informal trust of small teams harder to sustain. Without deliberate strategies to counter these forces, Agile transformations risk becoming agile in name only: process-heavy, coordination-poor, and trust-deficient.

10.4 Foundations for Scaling Trust

If trust doesn't scale by default, it must be scaled by design. This requires moving beyond interpersonal goodwill to structural enablers, cultural anchors, and intentional leadership. Trust at scale is an outcome of systems, rituals, and norms that consistently signal *you are safe here, you are seen here, and we are aligned.*

So what are the foundations upon which scalable trust can be built?

10.4.1 Shared Vision and Purpose

In complex Agile ecosystems, alignment begins with shared purpose. Teams don't need to know each other personally to trust one another. However, they must believe they are pulling in the same direction. A clearly articulated mission creates coherence across diverse workstreams, reducing the likelihood of misaligned efforts or conflicting priorities. When teams understand not just *what* they are building, but *why*, trust can emerge even in the absence of strong personal ties.

10.4.2 Mission Clarity Reduces Misalignment

Clarity is a trust accelerator. Ambiguity invites confusion and suspicion. Scaled environments must therefore double down on the crisp articulation of goals, roles, and expectations. Having a well-communicated mission gives teams the confidence to act autonomously, knowing their contributions align with the broader strategy. It also reduces the cognitive load of constant coordination, freeing teams to focus on delivering value, not decoding intentions.

10.4.3 Organisational Transparency

Opacity breeds mistrust. In scaled Agile environments, transparency is a practical necessity in addition to being a philosophical stance. Open decision logs, accessible product roadmaps, shared metrics, and visible governance structures foster a sense of inclusion and accountability. When decisions are visible, and are revisable, people feel respected and informed, not blindsided or second-guessed.

10.4.4 Psychological Safety at Scale

Creating psychological safety in a 5-person Scrum team can be a challenge; however, maintaining it across a 500-person program is another. Yet it is no less essential. At scale, psychological safety requires deliberate cultural engineering: setting norms for candour, framing dissent as a contribution, and designing forums where people feel heard, not judged. Retrospectives, all-hands meetings, and community of practice gatherings can be valuable, depending on how they're facilitated.

10.4.5 Candour in Large Forums

Teams will not be honest in large settings unless honesty is explicitly welcomed and rewarded. This means ensuring it is safe to give feedback. Leaders must actively normalise vulnerability, dissent, and uncertainty. Questions like "*What are we missing?*" or "*What's not working?*" need to be modelled, not merely tolerated. Only with intentional design can large meetings become spaces of shared learning.

10.4.6 Consistent Values Across Teams

Agile at scale succeeds when values travel across team boundaries. If one team lives by Agile principles and another reverts to command-and-control, friction is inevitable. The shared values of transparency, collaboration, and respect, act as cultural glue across diverse units. Frameworks help, but values are what keep the frameworks honest. They provide a common grammar for trust, enabling cohesion even when teams operate independently.

10.4.7 Agile Values as Cultural Glue

Agile's core values, as stated in the Agile manifesto: individuals and interactions, working software, customer collaboration, responding to change, are intended to be operational. At scale, they must become the DNA of decision-making. When teams know these values are more than posters on a wall, trust deepens. People begin to believe that the organisation means what it says and acts accordingly.

10.4.8 Leadership Modelling: Vulnerability and Integrity

Trust scales only if leaders lead it. Executive behaviour sends powerful cultural signals. When senior leaders admit mistakes, share uncertainty, or ask for help, they give permission for others to do the same. Vulnerability is the oxygen of psychological safety. Integrity, i.e. doing what you say you will do is its companion. Leaders who model both create an environment where trust can thrive both locally and systemically.

10.5 The Systemic Impact of Executive Behaviour

In scaled Agile environments, what executives *do* matters more than what they *say*. Teams watch leadership for cues: *Are priorities stable? Is feedback welcomed? Are cross-team tensions surfaced or buried?* Trust is either reinforced or undermined by these signals. A single act of transparency can resonate through the system; so, too, can a single breach of trust.

In conclusion, scaling trust requires both architectural thinking and cultural stewardship. It is the presence of clarity, transparency, safety, and consistent values that enables Agile to work at scale. These foundations, whist not eliminating the frictions of large systems, do create the conditions in which teams can move forward with confidence, even amidst uncertainty.

10.6 Structural Enablers of Trust at Scale

At its core, trust is relational, but in complex Agile ecosystems it must also be engineered. This means building systems and scaffolding that make trust not only possible, but also sustainable. This is especially valid when personal connection alone is insufficient. These structural enablers provide the visibility, coherence, and connectedness that allow trust to persist across boundaries of team, geography, or hierarchy.

Importantly, these enablers are not tied to any one single framework. Whether an organisation adopts SAFe, LeSS, Nexus, or a custom scaling model, certain patterns of coordination, visibility, and shared identity consistently support trust at scale.

10.6.1 Team-Of-Teams Architectures

Frameworks like Nexus, SAFe, and LeSS all acknowledge a simple truth: when many teams are working toward one product or outcome, coordination must be elevated to a new level. These architectures aim to retain Agile principles while supporting multiple teams through clear interdependencies, cohesive planning, and shared accountability.

In these models, teams do not operate in silos. They are treated as a team-of-teams, effectively a network that shares goals, rituals, and artefacts. This structure helps maintain alignment while preserving the autonomy of individual teams, which in turn builds inter-team trust.

10.6.2 Cross-Functional Coordination Roles

Roles such as Scrum of Scrums leaders, Release Train Engineers, or Integration Team leads act as trust brokers across teams. Their job is to surface impediments, clarify dependencies, and ensure that no team is left isolated. These roles foster relational continuity, ensuring that coordination is dependent on deliberate, institutionalised relationships.

10.6.3 Communities of Practice (CoPs)

Communities of Practice focus on craft, domain expertise, and social cohesion. CoPs bring together individuals across teams who share a skill set or discipline, such as QA, UX, DevOps, or product management. These communities become informal trust hubs, promoting cross-team knowledge sharing, mentoring, and identity-building.

Crucially, CoPs humanise the scaled enterprise. They remind individuals that while they may be one node in a large delivery network, they are also part of a supportive, like-minded professional community.

10.6.4 Transparency-Enabling Artefacts

Visibility is a prerequisite for trust. When people don't know *what* others are doing or *why* they are doing something, they fill the void with assumptions. To counter this, high-trust Agile organisations make use of artefacts that create systemic transparency. Examples of transparency enabling artefacts include:

- **Shared Backlogs:** Consolidated views of cross-team work can reduce duplication and surface interdependencies.
- **Visible Metrics**: Delivery metrics, quality indicators, and team health scores help teams self-regulate and foster mutual accountability.
- **Decision Records:** Open access to architectural and strategic decisions (e.g., ADRs) builds trust in how and why things change over time.

These artefacts signal inclusion and respect. They say, "You are trusted with the truth."

10.6.5 Rituals and Cadences for Synchronisation

High-trust environments run on rhythm. Synchronised planning, reflection, and delivery events create shared moments where alignment can be recalibrated and human connection re-established, even across vast systems.

Key examples include:

- **PI Planning / Big Room Planning:** these large-scale events allow teams to plan together, negotiate dependencies, and commit to shared outcomes. Done well, they generate alignment and camaraderie, in addition to commitments.
- **Joint Retrospectives:** reflection across teams builds empathy and allows systemic issues to surface.
- **System Demos:** regular demonstrations of integrated work foster transparency, cross-team appreciation, and feedback-rich environments.

When these rituals are consistent and meaningful, they create a rhythm that allows trust to flourish, even in high-change, high-complexity environments.

In short, structure shapes experience. Agile at scale succeeds when empowered teams are supported by systems that embed trust into the fabric of collaboration. When roles, artefacts, and rituals are designed with transparency, coordination, and learning in mind, trust becomes foundational.

10.7 Communication Patterns for Maintaining Trust

In any Agile environment, communication is the lifeblood of collaboration. But in scaled, distributed, or multi-team settings, *how* communication happens becomes just as critical as *what* is communicated. When communication breaks down, trust is often the first casualty. Conversely, well-designed communication patterns create a shared sense of reality, reduce uncertainty, and reinforce psychological safety.

At scale, trust is built through relationships, but it is maintained through communicative intent and design. The following patterns help teams stay aligned, informed, and confident in one another, even across complexity and distance.

10.7.1 Open Information Radiators

Information radiators which are visible, accessible artefacts like Kanban boards, Sprint goals, Burndown charts, or team health indicators, serve a dual purpose: they inform, and they reassure. When teams see each other's work and progress in real time, ambiguity is reduced and trust increases. Transparency signals integrity: nothing is hidden, and nothing needs to be.

In digital settings, tools like Jira dashboards, Confluence team spaces, and integrated reporting tools replicate the function of the physical whiteboard wall, keeping work visible and shared understanding alive.

10.7.2 Asynchronous Documentation

In large, often geographically dispersed environments, relying solely on synchronous conversation is unrealistic. High-trust Agile teams invest in asynchronous documentation, e.g. wikis, decision logs, and shared knowledge repositories, that allow team members to engage at their own pace, without losing access to key context or rationale.

Crucially, this isn't just about record-keeping. It's about building institutional memory and creating a durable, transparent narrative of *what decisions were made, why, and by whom.* This supports accountability and reduces friction when teams join, leave, or rotate across programs.

10.7.3 Synchronous Alignment Ceremonies

While asynchronous tools preserve context, synchronous rituals sustain connection. Events like iteration planning, Sprint reviews, and program increment (PI) planning create structured opportunities for real-time dialogue, negotiation, and feedback.

These alignment ceremonies reinforce mutual commitment and allow for course correction before misunderstandings calcify. They also offer critical opportunities for tone-setting. i.e. where trust can be built not just through *what* is said, but *how* it is said: with clarity, curiosity, and care.

10.7.4 Cross-Team Standups

Beyond team-level Daily Scrums, cross-team standups (often coordinated through a Scrum of Scrums or similar structure) provide a lightweight but powerful mechanism for surfacing interdependencies, addressing blockers, and reinforcing shared purpose.

When done well, these interactions reduce the "*us* versus *them*" mindset and help teams build trust across boundaries. When done poorly, for example, as a status-reporting ritual to leadership etc. they can inadvertently undermine it. The key is to keep the focus on team-to-team coordination, not upward accountability.

10.7.5 Channels for Open Dialogue

Tools like Slack and Microsoft Teams are often seen as productivity platforms. However, at their best, they function as digital trust ecosystems. Open channels enable spontaneous knowledge sharing, reduce the overhead of formal communication, and create spaces where cross-team empathy can flourish.

These platforms allow for levelling of access and informality in communication, which, especially in large or hierarchical organisations, can help bridge gaps in perceived power or visibility. When people feel they can contribute openly and be heard, trust grows.

10.7.6 Avoiding Information Hoarding and Gatekeeping

Few behaviours erode trust more quickly than gatekeeping. i.e. when knowledge, access, or decision-making authority is controlled by a select few. In Agile contexts, this often manifests as technical bottlenecks, undocumented processes, or exclusive meetings.

High-trust teams prioritise communication equity by making decisions visible rather than hiding them in private emails, ensuring that stakeholders are invited to discussions instead of limiting access, and documenting repeatable processes rather than centralising them in the hands of a few individuals. While gatekeeping may protect power, transparency is what truly safeguards trust.

Ultimately, trust at scale is a communicative achievement. It depends on intentionality, i.e. creating channels that are open, inclusive, and consistent. When teams can see the work, understand the decisions, and speak across boundaries, trust is more than just preserved, it is cultivated as an everyday norm.

10.8 Cultural Practices for Distributed Trust

Trust lives in culture in addition to organisational structures and rituals. When Agile teams are spread across geographies, functions, or time zones, culture becomes both more fragile and more essential. Without deliberate cultural practices, distributed environments can default to mistrust, misinterpretation, and fragmentation. But when trust is embedded in the way people speak, show up, and relate to one another, even across boundaries, it becomes self-reinforcing.

Distributed trust is undoubtedly a cultural challenge: how do we create a cohesive, psychologically safe environment when we're not in the same room, time zone, or sometimes even the same language group? Some practices to be considered include:

10.8.1 Normalising Vulnerability

Vulnerability is often associated with intimacy, small teams, and psychologically safe spaces, yet in scaled Agile environments it must be normalised at every level of the system to sustain trust across distance. When leaders openly share uncertainty and acknowledge that they do not have all the answers, they set a powerful tone that legitimises public learning and collective evolution, diffusing fear and creating space for honesty. Similarly, blameless postmortems function as a critical trust-building practice by allowing teams to examine failure without scapegoating, reinforcing the idea that learning is collective rather than punitive. When transparency about failure is modelled, particularly in larger or cross-team forums, it signals maturity and courage. In distributed systems, vulnerability thus operates as a cultural lever for alignment and trust.

10.8.2 Reinforcing Shared Language and Norms

In distributed environments, shared language functions as critical infrastructure; without it, teams may align on strategy yet diverge significantly in interpretation. Artefacts such as domain-specific glossaries, clear definitions of "done," and explicit working agreements establish a common grammar that supports coherence across teams. Team-level working agreements provide local clarity and alignment, while program or enterprise-level glossaries enable shared understanding across disciplines and regions. When designed thoughtfully, these artefacts, signal a collective commitment to clarity, mutual respect, and effective collaboration.

10.8.3 Building Empathy Across Sites

Empathy is a cornerstone of trust, yet it is difficult to sustain in purely virtual contexts, requiring distributed Agile cultures to deliberately design opportunities for its development. Practices such as team member rotations, even when short-term or symbolic, help individuals appreciate the pressures and realities faced by other teams or regions. Site visits and shared off-sites further foster human connection, dissolve stereotypes, and create shared experiences that strengthen future remote collaboration. Even virtual exchange rituals, including "day in the life" sessions or cross-site pairing, can build meaningful emotional bridges across digital divides. Empathy flourishes when teams shift from a mindset of "*they*" to "*we*," a transition that depends on contact and shared experience rather than collaboration alone.

10.8.4 Honouring Local Subcultures While Maintaining Cohesion

Global and distributed teams span not only geographic boundaries but also diverse cultural norms, communication styles, and work rhythms, making attempts to impose a uniform culture both unrealistic and counterproductive. Trust emerges from respectful coherence that acknowledges difference while fostering alignment. This requires recognising that local cultures shape how trust, authority, and feedback are expressed, while simultaneously cultivating global cohesion through shared values, rituals, and Agile principles that transcend local variation. The aim is cultural interoperability not homogeneity, i.e. a network of distinct subcultures connected by mutual respect and a shared sense of purpose.

In distributed Agile environments, trust becomes a cultural currency, which is earned through empathy, clarity, vulnerability, and inclusive norms. When cultural practices are intentional and human-centred, trust becomes distributed, just like the teams it supports.

10.9 Challenges and Anti-Patterns

Even the best-intentioned Agile transformations can fall into traps that quietly corrode trust. These anti-patterns are not always immediately visible. They often emerge subtly, as unintended consequences of scaling. Yet their cumulative effect can be profound, i.e. undermining psychological safety, fragmenting collaboration, and breeding disillusionment with the Agile promise.

Recognising these challenges is essential to cultivate organisational self-awareness which is a key condition for trust to take root and recover,

10.9.1 The Quiet Return of Command-And-Control

One of the most common anti-patterns in scaling Agile is the reassertion of command-and-control structures, cloaked in Agile terminology. As complexity increases, some leaders revert to familiar hierarchical habits, which can include demanding fixed roadmaps, enforcing top-down reporting, or centralising decision-making.

This may create the illusion of control, but it breeds mistrust. Teams sense when autonomy is performative and when accountability is punitive. True agility is incompatible with a culture of surveillance. Trust erodes when empowerment is replaced with enforcement.

10.9.2 Over-Standardisation that Stifles Innovation

Standardisation can be helpful for coordination. However, if t taken too far, it becomes a cultural straitjacket. When every team must follow the same backlog template, the same rituals, or the same tooling stack, regardless of context, local innovation and responsiveness suffer.

Worse, teams may feel that their unique needs or working styles are being ignored. This leads to disengagement, workaround cultures, or quiet resistance. Trust withers when teams are treated as interchangeable units rather than adaptive, intelligent agents.

10.9.3 Tooling Replacing Conversation

Agile tooling, e.g. Jira, Confluence, Miro, and the like, can support visibility and traceability. But when tools begin to replace human dialogue, trust will begin to decay. A comment on a ticket is not a substitute for a real conversation. An updated status field does not resolve tension.

In high-scale environments, it's tempting to rely on tooling to scale coordination. But trust isn't built through dashboards. Trust is built through connection, tone, and mutual understanding, which require conversation, not just configuration.

10.9.4 Opaque or Micromanaging Leadership

Trust cannot thrive in an environment where opacity or micromanagement prevail. When leaders withhold context, make decisions behind closed doors, or question team autonomy, they send a clear message: *you are not trusted.*

Micromanagement, in particular, signals fear and a lack of confidence in the system. It disrupts flow, undermines ownership, and discourages experimentation. The resulting atmosphere is one of compliance, exactly the opposite of what scaled Agile requires.

10.9.5 Loss of Psychological Safety in Large Forums

Large meetings, e.g. PI Planning, demos, leadership reviews etc. can either foster alignment or amplify anxiety. Too often, they become performative spaces where teams posture, play it safe, or say what they think leadership wants to hear.

When psychological safety is lost in these forums, honest dialogue disappears. Teams stop surfacing blockers or mistakes. Innovation stalls. Trust, once again, becomes the casualty. This happens because the environment penalises openness.

10.9.6 Fragmented Knowledge Sharing

In distributed or scaled contexts, knowledge becomes a critical organisational resource, yet without intentional knowledge-sharing practices it is easily fragmented and unevenly distributed. Critical insights may remain concentrated within a single team or individual, learnings from retrospectives may go undocumented, and architectural decisions may be shared informally or not at all. This uneven access to understanding creates confusion and resentment, undermining collective effectiveness. When some teams are perceived as being "*in the know*" while others are left in the dark, trust erodes both between teams and across the wider system.

In conclusion, scaling Agile without scaling trust leads to contradiction. Agile language may persist, but the spirit erodes. Recognising and actively countering these anti-patterns is a leadership imperative. Trust, once lost, is hard to reclaim. But when these traps are surfaced and addressed, organisations create the conditions not only for trust to return, but for agility to truly flourish.

10.10 Strategies for Leaders to Foster Scaled Trust

In scaled Agile environments, trust is a leadership artefact. It is shaped by what leaders design, enable, reward, and tolerate. As complexity grows, so too does the impact of leadership behaviour on psychological safety, cohesion, and cross-team confidence. Trust, in this context is a deliverable.

To foster trust at scale, leaders must move beyond vision-casting and oversight toward curating cultures of transparency, inclusivity, and mutual respect. The following strategies offer concrete ways leaders can catalyse and sustain trust across distributed Agile ecosystems:

10.10.1 Model Curiosity and Humility

At scale, leaders are rarely the closest to the work. This makes curiosity and humility essential leadership postures. When leaders ask open-ended questions; *What are we learning? What do you need from us?* they demonstrate trust in their teams' expertise.

Just as importantly, when leaders admit they don't have all the answers, they signal that uncertainty is a shared condition. This invites honesty, experimentation, and risk-taking, all of which are foundational to trust.

10.10.2 Invest in Transparency Infrastructure

Transparency needs to be engineered, requiring leaders to invest deliberately in systems that surface work, decisions, and metrics across teams rather than confining visibility within them. This includes providing open access to roadmaps, risks, and dependencies, maintaining shared dashboards that reflect quality, delivery, and team health, and creating decision records that explain not only what was decided but also the rationale behind those decisions. When such artefacts are visible, accessible, and regularly updated, they build confidence in the system itself and, critically, in the people responsible for leading and sustaining it.

10.10.3 Design Inclusive Communication Channels

Communication equity is essential for sustaining trust in distributed environments, requiring leaders to ensure that dialogue does not become concentrated within private threads, exclusive meetings, or opaque hierarchies. Instead, leaders should encourage the use of open Slack or Teams channels for discussions on delivery planning, quality concerns, and architectural decisions. They should normalise asynchronous updates so that time zones do not become sources of power imbalance, and they should invite rotating voices into leadership forums and planning ceremonies. Inclusive communication not only keeps people informed but, more importantly, signals that their contributions are valued and that they belong.

10.10.4 Sponsor Cross-Team Relationship-Building

Trust at scale depends on relationships that extend beyond individual team boundaries, and leaders play a critical role in legitimising and resourcing this relational work. This may include supporting cross-team pairing initiatives or job shadowing, facilitating shared off-sites and Retrospectives, and investing in deliberate community-building efforts such as internal conferences, unconferences, or "team-of-teams" showcases. By actively sponsoring these interactions, leaders signal that collaboration is not peripheral but central to the organisation's mission and success.

10.10.5 Reward Collaboration Over Local Optimisation

In scaled systems, what gets rewarded is what gets repeated, and when teams are incentivised to optimise local outputs at the expense of broader integration, trust between teams inevitably erodes. Leaders must therefore realign reward structures and recognition mechanisms to celebrate behaviours that advance systemic goals, such as teams that resolve cross-cutting blockers, individuals who contribute to shared artefacts or knowledge bases, and leaders who prioritise flow over siloed efficiency. For collaboration to endure, it must be made visible, genuinely valued, and materially recognised.

10.10.6 Keep Feedback Loops Intact Across Layers

As organisations scale, feedback is often lost in translation, filtered through layers of reporting or delayed until issues become unmanageable. Leaders must therefore actively safeguard and simplify feedback pathways by maintaining direct lines of listening to teams, such as through skip-level conversations or anonymous feedback channels, creating safe spaces for dissent where concerns can be raised without fear of reprisal, and acting visibly on the feedback received to demonstrate that listening leads to meaningful change. When feedback loops are fast, safe, and effective, trust grows organically; when they are broken, cynicism quickly takes hold.

In scaled Agile systems, leadership is about shaping the conditions in which teams can navigate complexity with confidence. Trust is the most precious currency in Agile. It is earned through presence, practice, and principled design.

10.11 Concluding Remarks

In remote and hybrid work, trust changes shape. It no longer rides on hallway conversations or casual glances across the team room. Instead, it travels through shared artefacts, inclusive rituals, empathetic communication, and principled leadership. Trust, in this digital-first world, becomes a deliberate design choice rather than an emergent by-product of proximity.

This chapter has shown that while remote and hybrid contexts introduce new frictions e.g. presence disparity, asynchronous drift, emotional invisibility etc., they also invite new forms of intentionality. Teams that succeed in building trust across distance do not wait for connection to happen organically. They manufacture moments of visibility, ritualise empathy, and engineer psychological safety into their day-to-day rhythms.

Leadership plays a decisive role in this transformation. In digital-first ecosystems, integrity is about making trust visible through action, especially when no one is physically watching. The best leaders are more accessible, more vulnerable, and more consistent in how they hold space for others.

Ultimately, the evolving nature of trust in remote and hybrid teams is a story of adaptation. What matters most is not where we work, but how we show up for one another. If trust is the invisible scaffolding of Agile, then in digital contexts, it must be intentionally and continuously reinforced with presence of mind.

The future of work is not less human because it is more digital. It simply asks us to practice trust more deliberately, design connection more carefully, and lead with empathy more courageously.

Reference

Tyagi, S., Sibal, R., & Suri, B. (2022). Empirically developed framework for building trust in distributed agile teams. *Information and Software Technology, 145*, Article 106828.

Chapter 11
The Evolving Nature of Trust in Remote and Hybrid Teams

Abstract Early Agile teams thrived in co-located environments where trust was reinforced through face-to-face interaction, informal communication, and shared physical context. As Agile work has shifted toward remote and hybrid models, these foundational assumptions no longer hold. Teams are now digitally connected yet often emotionally fragmented, with communication mediated through tools rather than proximity. In this context, trust must be deliberately designed and sustained. This chapter reframes trust as a dynamic, co-created outcome in digital-first Agile environments. It argues that trust in remote and hybrid teams is less dependent on physical presence and more grounded in shared purpose, consistent behaviour, psychological safety, and emotional resonance across distance. Drawing on research and practical experience, the chapter examines why trust fractures in distributed settings and explores how Agile practices must evolve to address asynchronous drift, reduced visibility of intent, and weakened social bonds. Through concrete patterns, rituals, and leadership strategies, the chapter provides guidance on cultivating authentic trust without co-location. It addresses challenges such as digital empathy, Zoom fatigue, distributed integrity, and equitable participation, offering a framework for sustaining trust as an intentional organisational capability. Ultimately, the chapter demonstrates that while work may be distributed, trust remains essential, and when thoughtfully designed, it enables Agile teams to collaborate effectively and resiliently at a distance.

11.1 Introduction

The earliest Agile teams thrived in environments where trust could be nurtured face-to-face, i.e. where quick glances, hallway conversations, and sticky notes on whiteboards provided constant cues of alignment and intent. In such spaces, trust felt natural, even effortless. But today, many Agile teams are no longer co-located. They are physically dispersed yet digitally interconnected, collaborating across cities, time zones, and continents. The office may be optional, but trust is not.

T. O'Connell, *Trust in Agile Teams*,
SpringerBriefs in Computer Science, https://doi.org/10.1007/978-3-032-21963-3_11

As work becomes increasingly remote or hybrid, the assumptions that once underpinned trust in Agile teams begin to falter. Familiar rituals: Stand-ups, Retrospectives, peer reviews, etc. still exist, but now they are filtered through video calls, asynchronous chats, and task boards. The result is a paradox because teams are more connected than ever yet often feel more disconnected. Communication is constant, but context is thin. Work is visible, but emotions are obscured. Presence is digital but not always felt.

This shift demands a reframing of trust as a dynamic, co-created outcome in digital environments. In remote and hybrid teams, trust does not emerge passively. It must be intentionally designed, sustained through new rituals, and encoded in how teams work, communicate, and care.

This chapter explores how Agile teams can adapt their practices to cultivate authentic trust without physical presence. It argues that trust in digital-first environments is transformed. It becomes less about proximity, and more about shared purpose, consistent behaviours, and emotional resonance across distance. It is less about what is seen, and more about what is felt, named, and honoured.

Through research grounded in practitioner experience, practical strategies, and team-level patterns, this chapter guides readers through the evolving architecture of trust in the age of hybrid work. From asynchronous drift to Zoom fatigue, from digital empathy to distributed integrity, this chapter will explore what it takes to work together at a distance and to truly trust one another there.

11.2 Reframing Trust for the Digital Age

Agile was developed in physical proximity. The manifesto's original authors met face-to-face, and its early practices, viz. co-located teams, osmotic communication, whiteboards covered in sticky notes, were all grounded in the belief that trust is easiest to build when people share time, space, and attention (Beck et al., 2001). But today, many Agile teams are physically dispersed yet digitally tethered, often collaborating across time zones, screens, and platforms. As the geography of work has changed, so too must our understanding of how trust is built and sustained.

Remote and hybrid teams operate in a context that is simultaneously hyperconnected and emotionally fragmented. Shared physical space, such as the spontaneous coffee chat, the impromptu problem-solving huddle, the ambient awareness of how colleagues are doing, is either radically diminished or completely absent. In its place, are video calls, task boards, group chats, and asynchronous updates. Tooling is abundant, but presence is mediated. Communication is continuous, yet often superficial. Meanwhile, the boundaries between work and personal life blur, and the lines between formal and informal interactions become less distinct.

In such contexts, traditional assumptions about trust no longer hold. Trust can no longer rely solely on face-to-face familiarity, real-time collaboration, or the subtle cues of in-person interaction. Nor can it be assumed that visibility of work equates to visibility of intent, mood, or engagement. In digital-first environments, trust must be made explicit through clear communication, psychological safety, and empathic rituals.

This chapter argues that trust in remote and hybrid Agile teams must be intentionally co-created. It is not a by-product of proximity but rather the outcome of deliberate design choices; choices that embed visibility, empathy, and relational intelligence into the very fabric of how work is structured, how leadership is enacted, and how teams connect.

Rather than lamenting the absence of co-location, we must ask: *How can we create conditions where trust thrives despite the distance?* This reframing invites us to reimagine trust as a distributed system which is one that is resilient, transparent, and emotionally intelligent by design.

11.3 Fractures and Frictions: Why Remote Trust Breaks Down

The transition to remote and hybrid work has revealed a difficult truth: trust is easier to erode than to sustain at distance. While distributed Agile teams can deliver value, innovate, and adapt, the social glue that holds them together is far more fragile in digital environments. Trust doesn't collapse all at once, rather it fractures along subtle, often invisible fault lines. If left unaddressed, these micro-fractures can compound over time, silently undermining collaboration, psychological safety, and team cohesion. Some of the issues that require vigilance include:

11.3.1 Asynchronous Drift and Delayed Empathy

In co-located teams, trust is reinforced through rhythm: the informal nod, the quick clarification, the instant feedback loop. In remote teams, communication often becomes asynchronous by necessity; delayed messages, out-of-hours replies, or long response times due to time zone differences can result in a significant impact. Over time, this introduces communication gaps (Bjarnason et al., 2011) or asynchronous drifting which encompasses the gradual divergence of understanding, context, and emotional resonance.

Without real-time connection, misunderstandings persist longer, tensions linger unaddressed, and empathy is delayed. A terse message may be interpreted as frustration; a silence may be mistaken for disengagement. Asynchronous workflows require discipline, but they also demand intentional empathy, or teams risk growing emotionally out of sync.

11.3.2 The Loss of Incidental Trust

In traditional workspaces, trust is usually built incidentally, through small, unstructured interactions. The hallway joke, the elevator chat, the shared lunch etc. all create a sense of familiarity and psychological closeness. These moments humanise colleagues, soften miscommunications, and build what sociologists call "thick trust" i.e. a trust rooted in personal connection, not just transactional reliability (Khodyakov, 2007).

Remote settings strip away most of these moments. Interaction becomes formalised: scheduled, bounded by agendas, mediated by tools. Over time, team members may become "functionally visible but emotionally distant." The absence of these micro-interactions weakens social fabric and reduces the margin for error when conflict arises.

11.3.3 Zoom Fatigue, Performative Presence, and Camera Anxiety

Video calls are often treated as a substitute for presence. However, they carry their own burdens. The constant self-view, lack of natural turn-taking, and absence of non-verbal nuance contribute to what is now widely recognised as Zoom fatigue. Over time, team members may feel they are performing presence rather than inhabiting it by nodding, smiling, and speaking in ways that look engaged without necessarily feeling connected.

Others may opt to remain off-camera due to anxiety, exhaustion, or environmental constraints. This introduces asymmetries in perceived participation. Those visible are presumed present; those invisible risk being interpreted as passive. In truth, visibility in video calls is a poor proxy for trustworthiness or contribution.

11.3.4 Presence Disparity and Psychological Safety

In hybrid teams, a more insidious challenge emerges i.e. presence disparity. When some team members are physically co-located while others are remote, unequal access to conversation, influence, and informal information flows can develop. Side conversations before or after meetings, impromptu decisions at a whiteboard, or social bonding over lunch are rarely captured in meeting notes or Slack threads.

This creates a two-tiered experience, i.e. one where remote team members often feel peripheral. When decisions are made without their input, or when their silence is interpreted as agreement, psychological safety deteriorates. People become reluctant to challenge ideas, raise concerns, or admit uncertainty. This occurs especially when people fear their contributions are less visible or valued.

These fractures and frictions don't arise from organisational malice or poor management. They are the by-products of a shift in how we work. Consequently, this shift calls for new rituals, new empathy, and new ways of seeing one another. Trust in remote and hybrid teams becomes harder to maintain. Recognising these failure points is the first step in repairing them.

11.4 The New Rituals of Trust: Practices that Work

In distributed Agile teams, trust must be ritualised to remain resilient. Without shared physical space, trust can no longer rely on serendipity or informal presence. Instead, it must be cultivated through intentional, repeatable behaviours such as rituals that foster visibility, belonging, and shared ownership.

These rituals are not decorative. They are design responses to the frictions and disconnections explored earlier. Done well, they keep people in trusting relationships in addition to keeping work on-track. Below are three key categories of trust-building practices that adapt traditional Agile sensibilities for the remote and hybrid age.

11.4.1 Ritualised Visibility

Remote teams do not need more meetings, rather they need more meaningful visibility. In the absence of hallway updates and informal cues, teams must surface work status and progress in ways that are transparent and humane rather than performative or bureaucratic. Daily stand-ups remain an important pulse-check, but in distributed settings they may shift to asynchronous formats, such as Slack threads or shared dashboards, particularly across time zones, with the intent always being to inform rather than report. Asynchronous updates, including end-of-day summaries or weekly reflections, enable team members to track progress and dependencies without adding unnecessary synchronous load. Similarly, status artefacts such as shared task boards, delivery forecasts, or blocker lists become trust-enabling when they are kept current and collectively owned. Together, these practices allow teams to see one another's work, progress, and constraints as an expression of accountability and care.

11.4.2 Micro-Moments of Connection

Trust grows not only from task alignment but from emotional resonance, and in remote environments this requires intentionally creating the small, humanising moments that no longer occur naturally. Informal digital coffee chats or "Donut" pairings provide space for connection outside the pressures of delivery, while check-ins that move beyond metrics, such as asking what is energising someone or how they are coping, invite emotional presence and surface unspoken needs. Emotion tagging through emojis or colour indicators in asynchronous tools can help convey tone and context where body language is absent, and virtual celebrations of milestones, birthdays, or team wins, when done with sincerity, help sustain team identity and morale. Though brief, these moments have a disproportionate impact, reminding teams that trust is built not only by delivering work together, but by feeling seen and valued together.

11.4.3 Equitable Participation

In hybrid and remote settings, who gets heard matters just as much as what gets said, and without intentional design some voices will inevitably dominate while others fade into the background. High-trust teams counter this by establishing inclusive norms that promote equitable participation across formats and contexts, such as adopting a "cameras optional, voice expected" approach that balances flexibility with presence. They make use of asynchronous ideation boards to allow people to contribute in their own time and style, which is particularly valuable across cultures, time zones, and personality types. Rotating facilitators in hybrid meetings further distributes ownership of team rituals and ensures that different perspectives shape how conversations unfold. Equitable participation is not merely a matter of good practice; it is a clear signal of psychological safety and a foundational input to collective trust.

In remote and hybrid teams, trust is a foreground practice. These new rituals do not attempt to replicate the physical office; they adapt to its absence by designing for connection, clarity, and cohesion in new ways. Over time, these seemingly small habits form the infrastructure of resilient, trusting teams, which are distributed, yet deeply connected.

11.5 Designing for Digital Empathy

In remote and hybrid teams, empathy is an operational imperative. Without physical proximity, teams lose many of the cues that signal distress, disconnection, or disengagement. A furrowed brow, a sigh, or a missed lunch are no longer visible in a virtual environment. As a result, emotional needs can go unnoticed, and psychological strain can silently intensify.

To maintain trust at a distance, Agile teams must design empathy into their workflows, rituals, and leadership behaviours. Digital empathy is about small, consistent acts of attunement that ensure no one becomes invisible.

11.5.1 Recognising and Responding to Struggling

Changes in behaviour, such as missing Stand-Ups, delayed responses, or unusually terse updates, can be early signals that someone is struggling. In co-located teams, these shifts are often noticed quickly and addressed through informal check-ins or quiet support. In remote settings, however, the absence of visible cues can lead to misinterpretation, with silence or delay incorrectly read as disengagement or lack of commitment. High-trust teams respond differently by creating norms that make struggle speakable. They normalise emotional check-ins at the start of meetings, provide private and non-evaluative spaces to raise workload or wellbeing concerns, and explicitly recognise that saying "*I need space today*" is a legitimate contribution. In doing so, these teams treat silence as a signal to reach in and connect, rather than pull away, making empathy a shared responsibility rather than solely a leadership trait.

11.5.2 Leading with Presence, not Surveillance

For leaders, digital empathy means being available without becoming invasive, particularly in distributed contexts where the boundary between attentiveness and micromanagement can quickly blur. High-trust leaders can demonstrate presence without pressure by investing in proactive one-to-one conversations that focus on the person rather than just the plan, by asking before advising, and listening without a hidden agenda, and by making themselves visible through invitation rather than demand, for example by saying "*I'm here if you want to talk*" instead of questioning why an update was missed. They also model emotional granularity by openly acknowledging uncertainty, frustration, or hope, creating permission for others to do the same. This steady, human form of leadership builds trust through vulnerability and consistency rather than control.

11.5.3 Reimagining Psychological Safety for Virtual and Hybrid Formats

Psychological safety remains the bedrock of trust, but in digital settings it must be consciously reimagined. Silence on a call does not necessarily signal agreement, a muted microphone may conceal discomfort, and the absence of challenge can reflect fear rather than consensus. High-performing remote and hybrid teams design for safety by ensuring that every voice is invited into the conversation, for example through round-robin sharing, and by framing disagreement as a valuable contribution rather than a disruption. They normalise uncertainty by making it acceptable to say, "*I'm not sure yet,*" or "*I need time to think.*" In hybrid contexts, teams also address presence disparity directly by giving remote participants the first opportunity to speak, appointing facilitators who actively notice who is being left out, and using anonymous input mechanisms in Retrospectives to surface concerns that might otherwise remain hidden. When psychological safety is intentionally designed in this way, remote and hybrid teams can become some of the most inclusive, reflective, and emotionally intelligent environments in which to work.

Digital empathy is the most deliberate expression of care. It requires us to notice what's missing, to question what's unspoken, and to create norms where people feel safe being fully human, even when their only presence is a pixelated square on a screen.

11.6 Leading with Distributed Integrity

In remote and hybrid Agile environments, leadership is measured by the integrity of one's actions at a distance. Distributed teams watch how their leaders behave, especially when no one is in the room. Integrity, in this context, becomes the operating system for trust.

To sustain trust across digital divides, leaders must show up differently: with vulnerability instead of certainty, clarity instead of control, and parity instead of privilege. These are actionable stances that shape how distributed teams experience inclusion, safety, and coherence.

11.6.1 Modelling Vulnerability When Remote

One of the most powerful things a leader can say in a distributed team is "*I don't know.*" When vulnerability is modelled well, it becomes a catalyst for trust rather than a liability, signalling that uncertainty is normal, questions are welcome, and learning is continuous, even in senior roles. In virtual environments, where tone is harder to read and status dynamics can be amplified, leaders must make intentional efforts to humanise themselves by admitting fatigue or challenge during check-ins, naming mistakes before others feel compelled to do so, and explicitly inviting dissent with questions such as "*What am I missing?*" or "*Who sees this differently?*" In remote contexts, where isolation and perfectionism often develop unnoticed, visible vulnerability creates a shared sense of reality and reassures others that it is safe to be genuine and imperfect.

11.6.2 Communicating Clarity Without Surveillance

Distributed teams crave direction, but direction must not be confused with micromanagement, and it is the responsibility of leaders to remain on the right side of this delicate boundary. Effective leaders focus on clarifying goals and giving teams the freedom to decide how work is delivered while remaining aligned on outcomes. They use transparent planning and asynchronous updates to maintain shared understanding without resorting to constant check-ins, and they trust teams with context by explaining the "*why*" behind decisions instead of reserving it for leadership-only forums. Surveillance, whether in the form of mandatory check-ins, granular time tracking, or excessive status reporting, signals mistrust and breeds compliance rather than commitment. Clarity, by contrast, enables autonomy. When people understand the destination and the boundaries, they are far better equipped to navigate complexity with creativity and confidence.

11.6.3 Creating "Remote-First" Parity

Perhaps the most overlooked leadership responsibility in hybrid teams is ensuring parity between remote and co-located contributors. Too often, decisions are made "in the room," with remote teammates included only after the fact, if at all, creating a second-class experience that quietly erodes psychological safety. Remote-first parity requires designing for inclusion by default rather than treating it as an accommodation. This means holding all key discussions in shared digital spaces even when some participants are physically together, ensuring that decisions never depend on hallway conversations, and using tools such as shared documents, digital whiteboards, and asynchronous voting that privilege contribution over physical presence. Far from being a procedural concern, this is a moral stance because everyone deserves equal access to influence, regardless of where they are located.

Distributed integrity means living one's values across distance. It is about consistency, honesty, and care in environments where leadership is often mediated by bandwidth and calendar constraints. In remote and hybrid Agile systems, trust in leadership is earned by design, not granted by position or title.

11.7 Trust: Beyond Presence to Shared Purpose

In remote and hybrid work trust has evolved. Unlike in co-located teams trust no longer depends on physical presence, shared desks, or spontaneous conversations. Instead, it flows through new channels: clarity of purpose, integrity of action, and emotional consistency across distance. What was once implicit in co-location must now be made explicit through design, empathy, and intention.

In distributed Agile teams, trust is built through shared intent. When team members know *why* they are doing what they're doing, and when they believe that others are aligned in that purpose. they can collaborate with confidence, even if they've never met in person. It is this alignment, not geography, that sustains cohesion.

Similarly, trust becomes more about reliability over time. Remote team members don't need constant oversight. Instead, they need to see that commitments are kept, that blockers are addressed, and that communication is timely and respectful. Consistency, not proximity, becomes the new currency of trust.

Perhaps most significantly, trust in digital-first teams becomes a matter of emotional resonance. Without casual cues or informal encounters, leaders and teammates alike must learn to tune into subtler signals, create space for honest expression, and treat empathy as infrastructure. Trust grows when people feel heard, respected, and safe to bring their full selves, even if they are reduced to a name in a chat window or a few pixels on a screen.

This is the paradox of remote work. The more our collaboration is mediated by tools, the more we must humanise our practices. Digital proximity alone does not create connection. But when supported by clear intentions, inclusive design, and empathetic culture, digital proximity becomes something more powerful, it becomes a platform for deep, distributed trust.

In this light, trust is something we architect, maintain, and evolve together. It is what transforms a set of individuals in different locations into a team with shared accountability, shared learning, and shared purpose.

11.8 Concluding Remarks

Remote and hybrid work illuminate the essence of trust. When the scaffolding of shared space disappears, what remains is a challenge: how do we stay connected, aligned, and psychologically safe when we are not physically together?

This chapter has explored how trust in distributed Agile teams is transformed. It no longer arises organically from proximity or co-presence. Rather it must be intentionally constructed. Trust in the digital-first workplace is a foreground discipline. It lives in the rituals we commit to, the language we choose, the systems we design, and the leadership we practice.

Rather than relying on spontaneous hallway chats or ambient awareness, remote teams must create visibility with care by making work transparent in ways that inform, not surveil. Human connection must be nurtured through micro-moments that acknowledge emotion and foster belonging, even when mediated by screens. Participation must be actively designed for equity, ensuring that every voice can be heard, not just those in the room or those most comfortable speaking.

Empathy, too, must be redesigned. In the absence of physical cues, teams must build norms that surface struggle, welcome vulnerability, and respond with compassion. Leadership must evolve from presence to principle. In distributed environments, trust in leaders is built not through proximity or oversight, but through integrity, humility, and consistency.

This evolution invites us to think differently. Trust is no longer about seeing someone at their desk; it is about seeing them as a person. It is less about checking in and more about checking with. In digital-first teams, trust becomes the architecture of collaboration. It is woven through shared purpose, reinforced through reliable communication, and sustained through mutual respect.

The future of Agile is not about replicating the physical office online. It is about designing for human connection in contexts where connection is no longer automatic. If we are willing to treat trust as a design responsibility as opposed to a cultural hope, then distributed teams can be built that are not only productive but profoundly connected. In this way, trust becomes the very thing that brings team members closer together.

References

Beck, K., Beedle, M., Van Bennekum, A., Cockburn, A., Cunningham, W., Fowler, M.,... & Thomas, D. (2001). Manifesto for agile software development.

Bjarnason, E., Wnuk, K., & Regnell, B. (2011, August). Requirements are slipping through the gaps—A case study on causes & effects of communication gaps in large-scale software development. In *2011 IEEE 19th international requirements engineering conference* (pp. 37–46). IEEE.

Khodyakov, D. (2007). Trust as a process: A three-dimensional approach. *Sociology, 41*(1), 115–132.

Chapter 12
Conclusion: The Competitive Advantage of Trust

Abstract In addition to their frameworks, tools and ceremonies, high-performing Agile teams are defined by the quality of trust, communication, and teamwork that underpin how they operate day to day. This concluding chapter synthesises the core insights of the book, arguing that these three foundations constitute a decisive and sustainable competitive advantage in modern Agile environments. When trust is present, teams collaborate openly, share knowledge freely, and adapt with confidence. When communication is clear, inclusive, and intentional, alignment improves and friction is reduced. When teamwork is treated as a shared responsibility rather than an individual trait, resilience and collective ownership emerge. The chapter translates these ideas into practical guidance for real-world Agile contexts, particularly those characterised by scale, distribution, and constant change. It highlights how trust, communication, and teamwork reinforce one another through everyday practices, leadership behaviours, and organisational design choices. The chapter concludes with actionable steps and reflective prompts to help teams and leaders strengthen these foundations intentionally. By prioritising these human-centred capabilities, organisations can move beyond mechanical Agile adoption and build environments where adaptability, innovation, and sustainable performance can thrive.

12.1 Introduction

Agile has never been just about speed. At its best, Agile is about learning faster, responding more intelligently to change, and enabling people to do their best work together. Yet many organisations discover that simply adopting Agile frameworks does not automatically deliver these outcomes. Stand-ups happen, backlogs are refined, and sprints are completed, but something essential is missing.

That "*something*" is rarely technical. More often, it is relational.

Trust, communication, and teamwork are the invisible foundations that determine whether Agile practices generate real value or become hollow rituals. When trust is weak, teams become guarded and risk-averse. When communication is unclear

T. O'Connell, *Trust in Agile Teams*,
SpringerBriefs in Computer Science, https://doi.org/10.1007/978-3-032-21963-3_12

or exclusionary, misalignment grows. When teamwork erodes, individuals optimise locally while the system suffers.

This chapter brings the book to a close by focusing on these foundations not as abstract ideals, but as practical levers for performance. It explores how organisations that invest deliberately in trust, communicate with intention, and treat teamwork as a shared discipline, consistently outperform those that focus only on process mechanics. In an environment defined by uncertainty, complexity, and continuous change, these human capabilities are the true source of Agile's competitive advantage.

12.2 Why Trust is the Real Differentiator in Agile Teams

Agile frameworks promise speed, adaptability, and innovation, but none of these qualities emerge from process alone. The true differentiator between teams that merely "do Agile" and those that consistently outperform lies in trust. Trust determines whether people speak up early, share incomplete ideas, admit uncertainty, and take responsibility beyond their job title. Without it, Agile rituals become mechanical and risk-averse; with it, they become engines of learning and momentum.

In high-trust teams, collaboration is not forced. Rather team members assume positive intent, rely on one another's commitments, and feel confident that mistakes will be treated as learning opportunities rather than failures. This creates the conditions for faster decision-making, reduced friction, and greater resilience when plans inevitably change. Trust lowers the cost of coordination and dramatically increases the quality of interaction.

Conversely, when trust is absent, teams compensate with controls, i.e. excessive documentation, approval layers, defensive communication, and rigid adherence to process. These behaviours slow delivery and drain energy, even when Agile ceremonies are faithfully observed. In practice, trust is a hard operational asset. Teams that invest in trust move faster because they spend less time protecting themselves and more time solving real problems together.

12.3 Communication as the Engine of Alignment and Learning

In Agile environments, communication is often confused with activity. Stand-ups happen daily, planning sessions are booked, reviews and Retrospectives fill the calendar, yet teams can still feel misaligned, frustrated, or quietly disengaged. The issue is rarely a lack of communication events, rather it is a lack of *meaningful* communication. Effective communication is about clarity, intent, and shared understanding. Often it is conflated with frequency of communication, but this is not necessarily effective communication.

High-performing Agile teams treat communication as a living system rather than a checklist of ceremonies. Information flows openly across roles and boundaries, not just upward or within silos. Decisions are explained rather than simply announced, allowing teams to understand the reasoning behind priorities, constraints, and trade-offs. Context travels with the work, so people know not only *what* is being done, but *why* it matters and *how* it connects to the bigger picture.

When communication works this way, coordination evolves into true collaboration. Teams anticipate dependencies instead of reacting to them. Misunderstandings are resolved early through conversation rather than escalation. Learning happens continuously, as feedback is shared in real time and insights are discussed openly rather than buried in reports or tools.

Strong communication also reinforces trust by reducing ambiguity. When priorities change or plans shift, transparency helps teams feel respected and included rather than surprised or sidelined. This clarity removes the need for second-guessing motives or navigating hidden agendas. In contrast, poor communication creates noise instead of insight i.e. updates become performative, difficult conversations are avoided, and critical signals are lost in dashboards and status reports.

Agile teams that communicate well are clearer, more deliberate, and more human in how they share information. Communication becomes the engine that aligns effort, enables learning, and keeps the team moving forward together.

12.4 Teamwork Beyond Ceremonies: From Process to Practice

Agile teams are often defined by their roles and ceremonies, i.e. developers, testers, Product Owners, Scrum Masters, Stand-ups, Reviews, and Retrospectives. While these structures matter, they are not what ultimately create high performance. Teams do not succeed because ceremonies exist, rather they succeed because people move beyond process and begin to operate as a cohesive unit with shared responsibility. Teamwork, in its strongest form, is a lived practice rather than a procedural checklist.

High-performing Agile teams function as collective systems rather than collections of individual contributors. Members see the success of the product and the team as a shared outcome, not something fragmented across roles or tasks. When bottlenecks arise, people step in regardless of job title. When risks appear, they are surfaced early. Ownership extends beyond "*my work*" to "*our delivery*." This kind of teamwork cannot be mandated through frameworks or enforced through metrics; it emerges where trust and communication are already embedded in everyday interactions.

Strong teamwork is also evident in how teams handle disagreement. Healthy teams do not avoid conflict. They engage with it constructively. Ideas are challenged without attacking individuals, and dissent is treated as valuable information rather than disruption. This is only possible when psychological safety is present, where team members believe they can speak honestly, ask for help, or admit uncertainty without fear of embarrassment or blame. In such environments, conflict becomes a driver of learning rather than a source of division.

When teamwork weakens, Agile rituals can continue but lose their meaning. Silos form even within a single team, people retreat into specialisms, and collaboration becomes transactional. Over time, delivery fragments and learning slows. By contrast, teams that invest in genuine teamwork gain resilience and adaptability as a group, allowing them to respond to complexity with cohesion rather than chaos.

12.5 The Hidden Cost of Low Trust in Agile Environments

Low trust in Agile environments often shows up quietly in everyday frustrations that practitioners recognise immediately but may struggle to name. Meetings feel heavier. Conversations become more guarded. People comply with processes while disengaging from outcomes. On the surface, Agile appears to be functioning, but underneath, the system is slowly losing its capacity to adapt.

One of the earliest signs of eroding trust is defensive behaviour. Team members begin to protect themselves rather than the work. Updates are framed to avoid blame rather than surface risk. Questions go unasked, and concerns are raised late, if at all. When trust is low, transparency feels dangerous, and silence becomes a survival strategy. The cost is not just emotional, it is operational. Problems surface later, when they are harder and more expensive to fix.

Communication also degrades in subtle ways. Information may still flow, but context does not. Decisions are announced without explanation. Changes arrive without warning. Teams spend more time interpreting intent than delivering value. Over time, this creates fatigue and cynicism. People stop assuming positive intent and start second-guessing motives, which slows coordination and weakens alignment.

Teamwork suffers next. Without trust, collaboration becomes transactional. Help is conditional. Knowledge is hoarded rather than shared. Individuals retreat into roles and specialisms, narrowing their focus to what feels safe and measurable. Agile ceremonies continue, but they lose their meaning. Retrospectives become superficial, planning becomes performative and learning stalls.

Perhaps the greatest cost of low trust is lost adaptability. Agile teams rely on openness, rapid feedback, and collective problem-solving to respond to change. When trust erodes, teams may still deliver, but they do so rigidly and defensively. Innovation slows, resilience weakens and change feels threatening rather than energising.

For practitioners, this is the real warning sign: when Agile feels harder than it should. Rebuilding trust is not about adding more process. It is about restoring honest communication, reinforcing shared ownership, and creating conditions where people feel safe to contribute fully again.

12.6 Trust, Communication, and Teamwork as a Reinforcing System

In high-performing Agile teams, trust, communication, and teamwork form a reinforcing system in which each element strengthens the others over time. When one is intentionally cultivated, it creates conditions for the others to grow. When one weakens, the entire system feels the strain.

Trust is the starting point, but it is sustained through communication. When people trust one another, they are more willing to speak openly, share incomplete ideas, admit uncertainty, and surface problems early. This openness, in turn, improves the quality of communication. Conversations become clearer, more honest, and more focused on learning rather than self-protection. As communication improves, misunderstandings decrease, alignment increases, and collaboration becomes smoother.

Strong communication enables real teamwork. Teams that communicate well coordinate implicitly, anticipate each other's needs, and adapt quickly when conditions change. They move beyond hand-offs and role boundaries toward shared ownership of outcomes. People step in to help not because a process requires it, but because the team's success feels collective. This shared experience of collaboration reinforces trust, as team members repeatedly see evidence that others are reliable, supportive, and committed to common goals.

Over time, this creates a virtuous cycle. Trust encourages open communication; open communication enables effective teamwork; effective teamwork generates successful outcomes and positive experiences, which further deepen trust. Learning accelerates because feedback is exchanged freely, improvements are acted upon, and knowledge is retained within the team rather than trapped in individuals.

Conversely, when one element erodes, the system destabilises. Low trust constrains communication, guarded communication weakens teamwork, and fragile teamwork undermines trust even further. High-performing Agile teams recognise that sustaining this reinforcing system is not accidental. It requires ongoing attention to how people relate, communicate, and collaborate from day to day, and from sprint to sprint. When nurtured deliberately, these foundations become a powerful source of resilience, adaptability, and sustained performance.

12.7 What High-Performing Agile Teams Do Differently

High-performing Agile teams rarely stand out because they follow the framework "better" than others. Instead, they distinguish themselves through consistent, visible behaviours that shape how work gets done and how people relate to one another. These teams feel different to work in. The difference is not charisma or heroics, but discipline, trust, and intentional human practices.

High-performing teams make work and decisions visible. They do not rely on insider knowledge or informal backchannels. Priorities, trade-offs, and constraints are openly discussed, and changes are explained rather than imposed. This visibility reduces speculation and second-guessing, allowing teams to focus energy on delivery rather than interpretation.

They talk early, not late. When something feels unclear, risky, or misaligned, it is raised quickly and informally. Small conversations replace big escalations. Because issues are surfaced while they are still manageable, these teams avoid the emotional and delivery costs of unresolved tension.

High-performing teams treat accountability as collective. Ownership does not stop at role boundaries. Team members step in when others are overloaded, notice when work is stuck, and feel responsible for outcomes rather than just tasks. Success and failure are shared experiences, not individual verdicts.

They handle disagreement with maturity. Differences of opinion are expected and even welcomed, particularly when decisions matter. Ideas are challenged without attacking people, and dissent is framed as contribution rather than disruption. This allows better decisions to emerge without damaging relationships.

They learn continuously and visibly. Retrospectives lead to action, not just reflection. Experiments are tried, reviewed, and either reinforced or discarded without blame. Learning is treated as part of the work, not an optional extra when time allows.

Finally, high-performing teams protect trust deliberately. They follow through on commitments, acknowledge mistakes openly, and repair missteps quickly. Trust is not assumed, rather it is maintained through consistent behaviour over time.

These teams are not perfect. But they are intentional. And that intentionality is what allows them to sustain performance, adapt under pressure, and work together with confidence and resilience.

12.8 The Role of Leaders in Sustaining Team Foundations

In Agile environments, trust, communication, and teamwork are shaped daily by leadership behaviour, decisions, and design choices. Leaders, whether they hold formal authority or informal influence, play a decisive role in determining whether these foundations strengthen over time or quietly erode.

12.8.1 Model the Behaviours You Expect to See

Teams take their cues from leadership far more from what leaders do than from what they say. When leaders are open about uncertainty, admit mistakes, and ask genuine questions, they legitimise learning and vulnerability across the team. When they listen without defensiveness and respond with curiosity rather than control, they create permission for honest dialogue. Conversely, when leaders default to blame, certainty, or micromanagement, trust contracts quickly. Leadership credibility is built through consistency: doing what you say you will do, explaining changes when they occur, and treating people with fairness and respect, especially under pressure.

12.8.2 Protect Psychological Safety and Team Integrity

High-performing teams require space to think, disagree, and experiment. Leaders must actively protect this space. This means intervening when blame replaces learning, when individuals are singled out rather than supported, or when delivery pressure starts to override sustainable ways of working. It also means resisting the urge to solve every problem on behalf of the team. Stepping in too quickly can undermine ownership and confidence. Protecting teams sometimes involves slowing things down, shielding them from unnecessary noise, or pushing back on unrealistic demands so that trust and focus are preserved.

12.8.3 Design Environments that Enable Good Teamwork

Trust and collaboration are strongly influenced by system design. Leaders shape these systems through how work is structured, how decisions are made, and how success is measured. Transparent goals, clear priorities, visible decision-making, and accessible information reduce ambiguity and friction. Incentives that reward collective outcomes rather than individual heroics reinforce teamwork. Regular forums for reflection, learning, and cross-team dialogue signal that improvement matters as much as delivery. Poorly designed systems force people into defensive behaviours; well-designed systems make trust the easiest option.

12.8.4 Create Conditions for Alignment, not Dependency

Effective leaders focus on alignment rather than control (Temitope, 2022). They provide clarity on purpose, boundaries, and constraints, then trust teams to determine how best to deliver within them. This balance enables autonomy without fragmentation. When teams understand the "*why*" behind decisions and see how their work contributes to broader goals, coordination improves naturally. Dependency on approval chains or constant oversight, by contrast, slows learning and weakens engagement.

Ultimately, leadership in Agile is less about directing work and more about curating the conditions in which teams can thrive. Leaders who model trust, protect psychological safety, and intentionally design for collaboration create environments where communication flows, teamwork deepens, and performance becomes sustainable rather than fragile.

12.9 Building for the Long Term: Sustainable Agility in Practice

Agility is often measured in speed: faster delivery, quicker feedback, and shorter cycles. Yet over time, teams and organisations discover that speed without stability is fragile. Sustainable agility is not about moving fast once, rather it is about continuing to move well as teams grow, people change, and complexity increases. Trust, communication, and teamwork are what make that possible over the long term.

As teams scale, the conditions that once supported easy collaboration begin to disappear. Informal conversations no longer reach everyone. Shared context fragments. New members join who were not present for earlier decisions. Without strong foundations, teams compensate by adding process, approvals, and controls. What starts as coordination quickly becomes bureaucracy, and agility quietly erodes.

Teams that invest early in trust, communication, and teamwork experience scaling differently. Trust reduces the need for excessive oversight because people assume positive intent and act responsibly. Strong communication preserves shared understanding even when work spans teams, time zones, or functions. Healthy teamwork ensures that collaboration extends beyond immediate delivery to include learning, mentoring, and collective problem-solving.

These foundations also protect teams through change. Reorganisations, shifting priorities, and personnel turnover are inevitable. Teams with weak foundations experience these moments as disruption. Teams with strong foundations absorb them as transitions. They adapt without losing cohesion because relationships, norms, and ways of working are resilient.

Sustainable agility is ultimately a long game. Tools, frameworks, and structures will evolve, but teams that continuously nurture trust, communicate with clarity, and practise real teamwork retain their capacity to adapt. In environments defined by uncertainty, these human foundations become the most reliable source of continuity, performance, and competitive advantage.

12.10 Final Reflections—Agility is Human Before It is Technical

Agile is often discussed in technical terms: frameworks, artefacts, roles, velocity, and tooling. These elements matter, but they are not where agility truly lives. Agility lives in how people relate to one another under conditions of uncertainty, pressure, and change. Long before Agile is a delivery model, it is a human system.

Throughout this book, one message has surfaced repeatedly, viz. trust, communication, and teamwork are the enabling infrastructure of effective Agile practice. When they are strong, Agile feels adaptive, energising, and resilient. When they are weak, Agile becomes brittle, procedural, and exhausting, irrespective of how faithfully the mechanics are followed.

For practitioners, this reframes where attention should be placed. Improving agility is about strengthening the conditions that allow people to think clearly together, speak honestly, learn continuously, and act with shared ownership. It is about designing environments where problems surface early, disagreements are safe, and collaboration feels worthwhile rather than costly.

As teams grow, distribute, and evolve, these foundations become even more critical. Processes can be copied. Tools can be standardised. But trust must be built, communication must be tended, and teamwork must be renewed continuously. They are living systems, not one-time achievements.

In the end, the most successful Agile teams are those that understand a simple truth: *agility is sustained by human connection.* When teams invest in how they work together, they create the conditions for lasting performance, meaningful learning, and work that people are proud to be part of.

12.11 Concluding Remarks

Agile has never failed because of a lack of frameworks. It falters when the human conditions required for those frameworks to work are ignored. At its core, agility is not a technical achievement but a social one. It depends on people trusting one another enough to speak honestly, communicate clearly, and work together toward shared outcomes rather than individual success.

Trust, communication, and teamwork are not "soft" concerns. They are hard advantages. Teams that cultivate them adapt faster, learn sooner, and recover more quickly from disruption. They waste less energy on defensiveness, misalignment, and rework, and more on solving real problems. In a landscape defined by uncertainty and change, these qualities become differentiators that competitors cannot easily replicate.

This shifts responsibility away from frameworks and back onto everyday choices. No scaling model, ceremony, or tool can compensate for low trust. No process can replace clear communication. No role definition can substitute for genuine teamwork. These foundations are created but can be undermined through how people listen, how leaders respond to dissent, how mistakes are treated, and how success is shared.

The challenge, then, is to practise Agile more honestly. To notice where silence replaces candour. To question where coordination has drifted into compliance. To ask whether teams feel safe enough to learn, as well as deliver value to the customer. Agility lives or dies in these moments. The question is not whether your organisation uses Agile practices, but whether it is willing to make the human choices that allow agility to thrive.

Reference

Temitope, A. O. (2022). Agile and organizational culture: Fostering agile values and mindset. *International Journal of Science and Research Archive, 7*(2), 672–681.

MIX
Papier aus verantwortungsvollen Quellen
Paper from responsible sources
FSC® C105338

If you have any concerns about our products,
you can contact us on
ProductSafety@springernature.com

In case Publisher is established outside the EU,
the EU authorized representative is:
Springer Nature Customer Service Center GmbH
Europaplatz 3, 69115 Heidelberg, Germany

Printed by Libri Plureos GmbH
in Hamburg, Germany